PhilanthropyRoundtable

BLENDED LEARNING

A Wise Giver's Guide to Supporting Tech-assisted Teaching

Laura Vanderkam

Karl Zinsmeister, series editor

Previous Guidebooks on Education Reform from The Philanthropy Roundtable

Saving America's Urban Catholic Schools
By Stephanie Saroki and Christopher Levenick

Investing in Charter Schools
By Public Impact

Achieving Teacher and Principal Excellence
By Andrew Rotherham

Current and Upcoming Wise Giver's Guides from The Philanthropy Roundtable

Karl Zinsmeister, *series editor*

For all current and future titles, visit PhilanthropyRoundtable.org/guidebook/.

Published by The Philanthropy Roundtable,
1730 M Street NW, Suite 601, Washington, D.C. 20036.

Free copies of this book are available to qualified donors. To learn more, or to order more copies, call (202) 822-8333, email main@PhilanthropyRoundtable.org, or visit PhilanthropyRoundtable.org. An e-book version is available from major online booksellers. A PDF may be downloaded at no charge at PhilanthropyRoundtable.org.

ISBN 978-0-9851265-4-4
LCCN 2013933142

First printing, April 2013

TABLE OF CONTENTS

PREFACE

A New Opening for Real Excellence

Few innovations in education today offer as much potential to transform how students are educated as the rise of so-called blended learning—the artful combination of computerized instruction (personalized for each student to make sure topics are mastered) with small-group teaching that is closer to tutoring than to traditional mass lectures. While so far put into practice in only a handful of schools around the country, some extraordinarily promising results have made this new style of pedagogy a source of great excitement for contemporary school reformers and donors working to improve education.

The pitfalls philanthropists face in addressing this crucial new frontier of learning are many. On the other hand, there may be no field in education where there are richer opportunities for brave and savvy givers to lead the education establishment toward a more excellent future. It is with the goal of supporting philanthropic excellence in this crucial new field that we publish this new guidebook by Laura Vanderkam.

Technology is not a panacea, and does not eliminate the need for skilled teachers and energetic administrators. When used in the intelligent new ways outlined in this publication, however, technology can bring impressive accomplishment to children previously mired in stagnation. And in this area, perhaps more than any other corner of America's huge education bureaucracy, strategic philanthropy can be the central catalyst for improvement.

> Here, more than in any other corner of America's huge education bureaucracy, philanthropy can be a central catalyst for improvement.

The key is to demand adaptive, rigorous, mastery-based student learning—not just expensive gadgets that do little more than collect dust. Donors who enter this wide-open field now and take the right approach can help teachers capture the promise of new technology that has so far eluded our schools.

In addition to being issued in book form, this work will also be distributed as an e-book and on the Roundtable website. It closes with a compilation of practical resources that will be useful to donors—including videos, reports, and leading blogs. We will keep these updated in the future. Visit PhilanthropyRoundtable. org/guidebook to find the freshest compendium of links.

As a next step, we hope you will consider joining The Philanthropy Roundtable and participating in the intellectually challenging, solicitation-free meetings we offer, entering our network of hundreds of top donors from across the country who debate strategies and share lessons learned. We offer customized resources, consulting, and private seminars, at no charge, for our members—all of whom are eager to make the greatest possible difference in their giving.

Please contact us at (202) 822-8333 or K-12@PhilanthropyRoundtable.org if you would like more information.

Adam Meyerson
President, The Philanthropy Roundtable

Dan Fishman
Director of K–12 education programs

Anthony Pienta
Deputy director of K–12 education programs

INTRODUCTION

"The first year, we tested the kids who came into high school. They tested on average at the 4th grade level. . . . At the end of that year, they were on average at the 8th grade level. In addition to these great results, their personalities changed. Since they know every day how they're doing, they start taking a real interest in improving."

—Frank Baxter, co-chairman, Alliance College-Ready Public Schools

"We are delivering real-time, relevant data to teachers that opens up new learning opportunities. . . . Before these technologies, there was a ton of data going into K–12, but not actionable data. We are actually affecting learning at the point of instruction."

—Jessie Woolley-Wilson, CEO, DreamBox Learning

"Technology is an amazing tool—it really is—but it's just a tool and if it's not used by good teachers in a strong school culture, it's not going to achieve what a philanthropist would want it to achieve."

—Scott Hamilton, co-founder, Seton Education Partners

"There are some things that teachers do exceptionally well that technology does very badly. There are some things technology does very well that are very time-consuming for teachers. . . . I don't ever want a teacher to grade another assignment again where there's a right and wrong answer."

—Brian Greenberg, CEO, Silicon Schools Fund

How New Technology and Savvy Philanthropy Might Combine to Transform Education

Education is an exciting—and growing—investment area for philanthropy. U.S. foundations give $5-6 billion per year to education,[1] and individual donors and corporations add billions more. Of course, even those significant sums are overshadowed by the hundreds of billions of dollars that localities, states, and the feds spend educating America's 50 million schoolchildren roughly. So in order to have an influence in a field that desperately needs reform, donors must spend carefully. They must target their money in smart and influential ways.

That's why many donors are interested in technology. Technology can bring dramatic change to the usual way of doing things. In basic economics, quality and cost are thought to move in the same direction. To get a better quality product, you generally need to spend more. When applied to education, this thought process has led to calls for smaller class sizes, nicer school buildings, more specialists and programs, and higher teacher pay. All of these types of increased expenditure have been employed heavily over the last two decades.

Current American educational spending is both very high compared with our own history, and much higher than nearly all other rich countries. In constant, inflation-adjusted dollars, U.S. educational spending per pupil per year increased from $5,718 in 1980-1981 to $10,694 in 2008-2009. That near doubling, however, and the approximate quadrupling of spending since 1960[2] have not produced commensurate quality gains. Indeed, the attempt to spend our way to better schooling has produced astonishingly few positive results of any measurable sort. There are blockages in our educational system, and variables beyond money that have to be overcome if today's mediocre results are going to be improved. In any case, given our new era of tight budgets, bankrolling further high-cost improvements is not possible.

Technology, however, can sometimes undo the traditional equating of better quality with higher costs. Today's mobile phones are both far superior and much cheaper than the brick-sized models that real-estate agents used in the early 1990s. Each new generation of computers does more

---

1. Foundation Center, "FC Stats: Funding by Subject Area," http://foundationcenter.org/findfunders/statistics/ gs_subject.html. About half of this goes to K–12 education, the other half to higher education.
2. U.S. Department of Education, National Center for Education Statistics, *Digest of Education Statistics, 2011* (NCES 2012-001), Table 191, http://nces.ed.gov/fastfacts/display.asp?id=66.

> Can technology improve student outcomes while also lowering costs? The answer should be yes.

while costing less than the one before it. This progress raises the question: Could technology do the same for education? Can technology lower costs and improve student outcomes?

The answer should be yes. In three decades of trying, though, educators have not succeeded in capturing the productivity gains that technological progress has introduced into other fields. "This is the 21st century, and we're not using technology very intelligently at all in schools," complains Eli Broad, one of today's most aggressive education donors and reformers. Having access to technology and applying it effectively turn out to be two different things. "We've got to start taking advantage of blended learning by using technology more effectively in classrooms," Broad urges in an interview with *Philanthropy* magazine.

In addition to opening new doors and saving us money, technology has recently done one other very important thing to the parts of American society that have been receptive. It has allowed dramatically *personalized* products and solutions to evolve quickly, to serve and satisfy people in as many different ways as there are different appetites, learning styles, and human passions. The era of one-size-fits-all is over.

There are hints that the new opportunities, economic efficiencies, and personalizing power of technology may finally be starting—just starting—to transform the process of teaching children today. As some of the quotations at the start of this guidebook suggest, new ways, methods, and results are beginning to change the old ways of doing things. People who study innovation call these changes "disruptive"—a word that sounds negative, but in this case means something laudable. A disruptive technology upends the status quo in a way that can yield dramatic improvements in our quality of life which might otherwise take generations to evolve. The car disrupted the horse and buggy. Email has disrupted the postal mail business. In education, we are seeing promising glimmers of disruptive alternatives to rote worksheets, lowest-common-denominator lectures, disengaged students, burned-out teachers, and an educational ecosystem where even hard work changes nothing by itself.

In this book, we'll briefly explore why we're still only in the early stages of the educational technology revolution. Then we'll look at how some innovative schools and other organizations are pioneering new methods of personalized learning built on new technology. Today's most promising experiments combine computerized instruction with immediate assessment and feedback, and are carefully linked to the best of traditional classroom teaching practices.

That mix of digital and human elements is what makes the "blend" in blended learning. Today's push is to make the most of teacher time by deploying educators as tutors and mentors who focus on the precise concepts that each student is missing, without holding back those who are ready to move ahead, and without abandoning those who need supplemental instruction on concepts they haven't yet mastered. This dramatically different style of instruction—variously referred to as "blended learning," "hybrid instruction," or "personalized learning"—attempts to optimize the combination of empowering technology and human touch. And there are indications that it might not only be helpful for students who get lost in today's mass-lecture model of teaching, and a relief for heavily burdened teachers, but also an answer to the spiraling costs of conventional schooling that have become such a drag on families and communities.

We'll look at the early results in schools that are experimenting with blended learning. We'll look at more revolutionary concepts still on the horizon. We'll examine the roadblocks and challenges impeding breakthroughs. And we'll look very specifically at how philanthropists can assist in bringing these promising new methods to children desperate for better ways of learning. It's clear that private donors are the most important force in cajoling today's sluggish public education bureaucracy to be receptive to the positive "disruptive" power of blended learning. "Smart philanthropy is the key to making sure that technology is used in game-changing ways to empower teachers, improve curricular content, customize learning opportunities for every child, and do all this at an affordable cost," says Adam Meyerson, president of The Philanthropy Roundtable.

It's a tall order. And blended learning is still very much in its early days, so sensible observers will be careful not to over-promise. But there is reason to hope that new technology can help America finally deliver on its promise to educate every child to a high standard. It's possible that intelligent software, flexibly employed by wise educators, pushed by savvy philanthropists and a demanding public, could finally provide a way to accomplish what we all know needs to be done in public education.

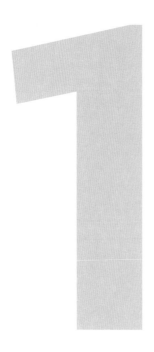

What Exactly Is Blended Learning?

According to a summary by the Innosight Institute, a California think tank founded by Clayton Christensen, Michael Horn, and Jason Hwang, there are several crucial elements that combine to comprise "blended learning." They define the practice this way:

> A formal education program in which a student learns at least in part through online delivery of content and instruction with some element of student control over time, place, path, and/or pace, and at least in part at a supervised brick-and-mortar location away from home.

This definition is loose enough to leave room for many different kinds of programs.

It can encompass a teacher experimenting with fresh methods on his own. Harsh Patel, a Teach For America corps member assigned to a charter school on the south side of Chicago from 2010 to 2012, learned about Khan Academy (which we'll discuss in detail later) when he was a college student. Patel then used it in his own math classes. He had kids watch Khan's instructional videos at school and at home, then rotate through stations where they put in computer time doing Khan problem sets, undertook group projects, or experienced small-group instruction with the teacher.

The Innosight definition can also encompass a whole-school model of blended learning, of the sort we'll look at more deeply in the next few chapters. Rocketship Education, some of the Summit Public Schools, some of the Alliance College-ready Public Schools in Los Angeles, KIPP Empower Academy in Los Angeles, and other places are transforming entire schools into blended-learning institutions.

Different observers use different descriptions and breakdowns, but four basic strands of blended learning are often identified:

- **Group Rotation:** Students move, in groups, between different learning stations (e.g., teacher-led sessions, solo work online, small-group collaborations), either on a fixed schedule or at the teacher's discretion. *Example:* KIPP Empower Academy in Los Angeles serves about 40 students per class.

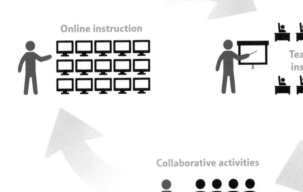

- **Individual Rotation:** Most instruction is delivered online in an individually customized way, with teachers' aides circulating to offer help. Teachers hold small tutoring sessions. Students rotate when the teacher or their computer results call for a new learning mode. *Example:* Carpe Diem School in Yuma, Arizona, serves approximately 300 students in grades 6-12.

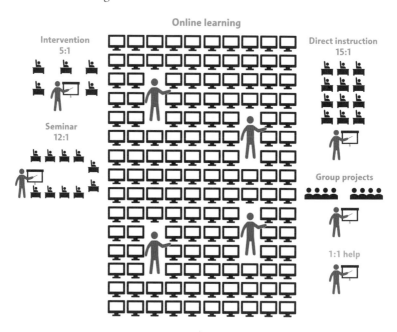

- **Self-mixed:** Students attend traditional classrooms with conversational teacher-led group instruction, but supplement this with one or more courses online, taken either during school or outside of school. *Example:* Growing numbers of public schools.

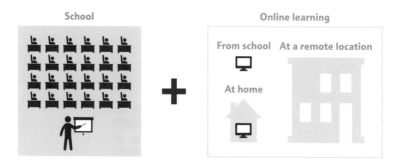

- **Online + Enrichment:** Students are enrolled in a full-time virtual school, with options to meet with instructors periodically for tutoring, exams, or enrichment. *Example:* Florida Virtual School. Nationwide, 250,000 students were enrolled fulltime in online schools during 2010-2011.

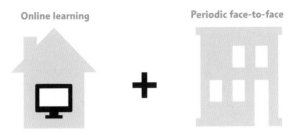

Educational entrepreneurs are still trying to figure out what works best for different kinds of students, and in which settings. The growth of blended learning over the past few years has taught reformers a lot, and given them glimpses of the possibilities yet to be fully realized.

The language is changing as the field develops. Even pioneers aren't sure that "blended learning" is the right umbrella description. "Personalized learning" better captures the way that the new technology can transform instruction from one-size-fits-all mass lecture to individualized lessons that let all pupils find the pace and style of instruction that helps them to their best results. Diane Tavenner, head of the Summit Public Schools, prefers "optimized learning." She says it "captures what's missing with 'blended' and 'personalized' . . . the power of data and analytics and feedback." Another common shorthand is "digital learning," but some proponents worry that it puts too much emphasis on technology as a good in itself. Technology is simply a tool to achieve a different, and better, interaction between pupils and teachers.

This is an ongoing discussion. In this guidebook, though, we will use the term "blended learning," and follow the basic definition from the Innosight Institute outlined above. In plain English, blended learning involves using technology and human teachers in combination to achieve better results than either could produce on their own. Both technology and teachers can play to their strengths. Computerized instruction delivers individualization and immediate feedback. Teachers turn into tutors and mentors, producing in one-on-one moments with students those insights that make teaching the rewarding career it can and should be.

Why Technology Hasn't Changed Education Yet
You can forgive experienced educators for being jaded when they hear

talk of revolutions. Schools are full of expensive knick-knacks that were going to change everything. Plenty of schools have high-tech white boards, closed-circuit TV, projectors, laser disc players, and ever since the early days of computers there have been rows and rows of them in schools, sitting in separate labs, or the library, or in sets of three in the back of classrooms, often looking forlorn and two years behind whatever commercial models kids are using at home. Lots of schools convinced themselves that simply giving every child a laptop was going to supercharge their pace of learning—which was both fruitless and expensive as educational mistakes go. According to Clayton Christensen, Michael Horn, and Curtis Johnson's *Disrupting Class: How Disruptive Innovation Will Change the Way the World Learns*, the U.S. spent $60 billion up to the time of their book's 2008 publication—and doubtless a lot more since—putting computers in classrooms, without any discernible breakthrough in student performance.

Even savvier ways of turning kids' love of staring at things on screens into learning quickly reached natural limits. Most 30-somethings can recall doing writing exercises on early Apple desktops in the 1980s, playing Oregon Trail on rainy elementary-school days, or drilling on MathBlaster. Many of these software packages were great products, but they didn't turn out to be transformative in the sense of changing how school worked.

As the internet became a part of everyday life, people became interested in online learning—how lessons could be delivered remotely, in an updated version of the correspondence courses students have always taken. Many of these courses have become quite advanced and interactive. Coursera, a company founded by two Stanford professors, now offers lectures from top universities to thousands of students for free. Courses include fantasy and science fiction from the University of Michigan, and quantum mechanics and quantum computation from the University of California, Berkeley. Far from offering simple video versions of live presentations, these courses flit between demonstrations and lectures, and ask students frequently for updates on their comprehension.

In a lower-budget vein, former hedge-fund employee Sal Khan in 2004 began producing what eventually became thousands of videos on math, science, and now humanities topics, originally for his young cousins. He posted them online, where anyone can view them for free. To date, Khan's lessons have been screened more than 230 million times—though his real innovation may be his problem sets, which we'll discuss later in this guidebook.

Online and virtual learning has been a boon for a number of different constituencies:

> A careful mix of digital and human elements—
> advanced computerized instruction linked
> to the best of traditional teaching—is what
> makes the "blend" in blended learning.

Families that are home schooling. Millions of American children are now educated at home rather than in an institution. Just from 1999 to 2007, this form of schooling increased its market share from 1.7 percent of K–12 children to 2.9 percent. If mom or dad need help explaining a topic, they just summon up Sal Khan or some similar curriculum for a different take.

Children who can't or don't want to attend a traditional school full-time. The majority of states now offer virtual schools for kids who want or need to learn this way for some reason: the child is an Olympic-caliber gymnast who's training eight hours per day; the child is hospitalized long-term after a car accident; the household is located in a remote region; a family wants their child to go to school part-time and learn at home part-time.

Florida Virtual School, which we'll explore later in this guidebook, is a leader in this field, offering K–12 classes ranging from Latin and Chinese to art history and forensic science. The school is compensated in an innovative way: it gets paid if and when a student completes a course, a concept that on its own could spark new motivation in education. An amazing 40 percent of Florida children now take at least one class through Florida Virtual School, and virtual schooling is also growing fast in other parts of the country. The International Association for K–12 Online Learning, known as iNACOL, reports that 275,000 students were enrolled full time in online schools during the 2011-2012 school year.

Children getting left behind. There are promising applications of online schooling for "credit recovery"—the educational euphemism for when students fail a class and need to take it again. Many of today's options for repeating a class are very low in quality, so there is big potential upside here. State virtual schools are getting into this area, as are some commercial operators.

Children who want more variety or challenge. Online learning means that students can take courses that a local school doesn't offer. This is certainly beneficial for students in rural areas or small schools who otherwise wouldn't have access to a full suite of Advanced Placement classes, or foreign languages beyond the ubiquitous French and Spanish. Some teenagers are ready to pursue college credits online at the same time as they are finishing their high school degrees.

Today's newest technology allows dramatically personalized solutions to evolve quickly.
The era of one-size-fits-all education is over.

This ability to enrich educational programs is one factor driving the growth of state virtual schools. Several Philadelphia-area Catholic schools have combined forces to offer advanced math to their students by broadcasting a teacher from one school into the others. The teacher can see all the classes on her dashboard, and the camera pans immediately to any student who speaks up with a question. The 2012 *Keeping Pace* report estimates that more than 5 percent of all K-12 students in the U.S.—several million children—now take at least one virtual course on line in the course of a school year.

Many of these virtual-learning options have face-to-face components: Florida Virtual School students can go on field trips, and talk by phone with their teachers. With enough face-to-face interaction, some virtual schools might qualify as blended-learning programs, and students enrolled in online courses as a supplement to traditional ones fit into the "self-blend" model. But pure online learning bumps into the question of whether technology is simply using new piping to further the existing model of teaching, or whether it's changing how content is delivered and assessed in a way that is more effective than what isn't working now.

In theory, online learning is revolutionary. Lectures on any topic can come from the very best teachers. The Civil War was better explained by Shelby Foote than by your high school history teacher who took one class on the topic 20 years ago. An online lecture on the quadratic equation, or the *Mona Lisa*, can be tested for effectiveness by hundreds of thousands of people before you watch it, so you'll know for sure that it's good.

Technology democratizes access to excellence. A high-school student, a prisoner, a displaced auto worker brushing up to go back to school, and a kid in the Australian outback can all hear the best lecturers. It's much like the way recording technology gave everyone access to the opera singers and symphonies that you once could hear only if you lived in a big city and had the money for concert tickets.

On the other hand, listening to a lecture—in whatever form it comes—is not all that innovative. Yes, even the most average online lecture will generally be better than what the bottom half of America's classrooms feature. Schools are rife with stories of teachers simply writing bullet points on a board for students to copy down, or teachers having students take turns reading aloud from the text book, paragraph by paragraph, for mind-numbing weeks. But the high-quality teachers that do exist in schools have a lot to offer beyond what a student could get by watching a lecture and then answering questions about it.

Pure online learning also bumps into logistical issues when it comes to children. While online learning means there's less necessity to go to a school building to get an education, most parents want to send their kids to a physical school. School serves a social and child care function apart from pure learning. Parents want their children somewhere safe and staffed by competent adults while they're at work. Since schools are paying for physical space and competent adults, they figure they should use those competent adults to offer something more than the modern equivalent of correspondence classes.

So that raises the question: how can technology augment what good teachers do? How can technology help teachers get better results and make their jobs more satisfying? If blended learning can combine the best of online and in-person education, it will be something new and powerful. And that is why knowledgeable observers are so excited.

The Essential Preconditions for Change

The reason donors care about education, in competition with the world's myriad other woes, is that schools are the engines of opportunity. Get this investment right, and you reap dividends in human capital that few other categories of philanthropy can match: happier people, more prosperity, even things like better health outcomes as levels of education rise. Not to mention a stronger and more successful nation.

There's plenty of evidence that most American schools aren't getting their educational investments right at present. Every few years, a new wave of lackluster scores on international comparison assessments such as the TIMSS (Trends in International Math and Science Study) and PISA (Program for International Student Assessment) leaves Americans burying their heads in their hands. The PISA exam tests several thousand 15–16 year olds from a variety of countries in different subjects. U.S. students ranked 24th out of 29 industrialized nations in math in 2003. In 2006, U.S. scores in science were lower than the average score in 22 other lands, and lower than the average in 31 other places when it came to mathematics.[1] In 2009, the PISA expanded to include more countries. The good news is that the U.S. came out ahead of developing nations such as Uruguay and Azerbaijan. The bad news is that the U.S. didn't move up in the rankings from its earlier middling scores. In 2009, the U.S. was 31st in math, 23rd in science and 17th in reading. Figures released in late 2012 from the 2011 TIMSS found that some progress had been made in fourth-grade reading, math and science, with U.S. elementary schoolers placing sixth out of 60 countries in reading and ninth in math. The discouraging news is that the rankings were considerably lower for eighth graders, meaning that the U.S. school system, rather than turning out globally superlative scholars, makes students less competitive the longer they stay in it.

When Americans hear these numbers, they assume these rankings are the result of failing urban schools. Certainly, the statistics associated with such schools are bleak. Only 52 percent of young black men graduate from high school in four years, as do just 58 percent of young Latino men.[2] Students who drop out will later have trouble supporting themselves and their families; 44 percent of high-school dropouts under age 24 are jobless.[3]

It's a serious mistake, though, to think that educational mediocrity hasn't infiltrated our well-funded suburban schools too. Some do all right, but even "good" schools generally aren't that good from an international perspective. An April 2009 McKinsey report on the economic impact of achievement gaps reported that compared to their counterparts abroad, America's top 10 percent of students ranked 25th out of 30 on PISA math results—not that different from overall results. Indeed, the scores of the top 10 percent of students in the U.S.—those students

1. U.S. Department of Education, Institute of Education Sciences, Program for International Student Assessment, 2003 results, *List of Figures: Mathematics*, http://nces.ed.gov/surveys/pisa/pisa2003highlightsfigures.asp?Quest= 1&Figure=9; Institute of Education Sciences, Program for International Student Assessment, *A Summary of Findings from PISA* 2006, http://nces.ed.gov/surveys/pisa/pisa2006highlights.asp.

2. Schott Foundation for Public Education, "The Urgency of Now," 2012 report on public education and black males, http://www.schottfoundation.org/urgency-of-now.pdf.

3. The Broad Foundation, "Education," http://broadeducation.org/about/crisis_stats.html.

who might qualify for gifted programs—would be considered middle-of-the-pack in top-scoring countries like South Korea, Finland, and Belgium.[4]

In a globalized world, it is no longer enough to be competent by the standards of one's local economy. American students will compete globally, and only a small fraction have the skills to thrive in a world where not just manufacturing jobs, but even routine mid-skilled jobs can be outsourced to lower-wage countries, and where countries such as China and India have their own intellectual elite.

The problem of educational stagnation has been debated at length during the three decades since the report *A Nation at Risk* warned of a "rising tide of mediocrity." Explanations abound for why we're so mired in underperformance, even in schools serving mostly intact and economically successful families, and why we are doubly failing in schools facing the family woes endemic to high-poverty districts. These explanations differ depending on people's politics and personal experiences, but what we do know for sure is that the American education system is plagued at all levels by chronically low expectations.

And, to repeat, America spends more per pupil than the other developed countries to achieve these unimpressive results. If spending isn't the solution, what is? Clear-eyed donors and reformers have followed two routes toward change: expanding choice and introducing accountability. These factors are what improve quality and outcomes in other parts of American life. They are just as important in schooling.

School choice and the accountability movement have shown exciting potential. However, neither strategy has so far managed to create widespread breakthroughs in achievement. Yet choice and accountability have created conditions that allow the rise of alternatives like blended learning—which may turn out to be more viral, more disruptive, and more widespread, ultimately yielding educational improvements that are broadly effective and unable to be blocked, even by the most stubbornly resistant parts of today's educational establishment.

School Choice

The first wave of school reform focused on giving families options. School choice is rooted in the same theory of competition that governs and hones the rest of our economy. If schools have to compete for children, market disciplines will force them to improve themselves.

Nobel Prize–winning economist Milton Friedman envisioned a voucher system in which parents could spend their children's publicly allotted school funding at whatever institution appealed to them, so long as it met minimum

---

4. McKinsey & Company, *The Economic Impact of the Achievement Gap in America's Schools,* April 2009, http://mckinseyonsociety.com/downloads/reports/Education/achievement_gap_report.pdf.

standards. A number of cities—such as Milwaukee and Washington, D.C.—have tried voucher programs, but they've had to drag political opponents every inch of the way.[5] Consequently, charter schools have outpaced vouchers as a form of (much more limited) school choice. Charter schools have been the focus of many major philanthropic investments since Minnesota passed the first law in 1991 allowing outside groups to "charter" schools that would operate independently from central district authorities.

Charter schools are public schools, supported by public dollars (aided, sometimes, by fundraising), but they have more flexibility than traditional schools. As a practical matter, this often means that school leaders can choose their own staff. Teachers at many charter schools are not unionized.[6] School leaders can experiment with variables like the length of the school day and—critical for blended learning—different formats of instruction and different class sizes.

It's a serious mistake to think that educational mediocrity hasn't infiltrated our well-funded suburban schools too.

If charters are undersubscribed, or underperforming, they can be shut down—thus adding market discipline as a condition of freedom. This probably needs to be done more often in the future than it is right now—a study from the National Association of Charter School Authorizers found that the percentage of schools being denied charter renewals has been declining over time. In the school year ending in 2009, 13 percent of charters that came up for renewal were shuttered; in 2010, 9 percent were; and in 2011, just 6 percent were closed.[7] This could indicate that charter quality is improving, but one 2009 study from Stanford found that 37

---

5. The National Education Association (NEA) teachers union is explicitly against vouchers, claiming that "they divert essential resources from public schools to private and religious schools, while offering no real 'choice' for the overwhelming majority of students."

6. The NEA is more neutral on charter schools. "NEA believes that charter schools and other nontraditional public school options have the potential to facilitate education reforms and develop new and creative teaching methods that can be replicated in traditional public schools for the benefit of all children," the official position reads. However, "[c]harter schools should be subject to the same public-sector labor relations statutes as traditional public schools, and charter school employees should have the same collective bargaining rights as their counterparts in traditional public schools."

7. National Association of Charter School Authorizers, The State of Charter School Authorizing, 2011, http://www.qualitycharters.org/press-releases-statements/national-survey-shows-charter-school-closure-rates-dropped-in-2010-2011-school-year.

percent of charter schools produced worse test scores than their traditional counterparts.[8] If that's the case, then the non-renewal rate should be closer to 37 percent
to show the system is working.

Of course, among traditional public schools, the proportion of poor performers closed each year is close to zero. And charters are coping with more
than their share of difficult students—many enrollees are students who had
serious problems in their previous schools. Meanwhile, good charter schools
do so well that they are massively oversubscribed. The heartbreaking lottery
scene in the 2010 documentary *Waiting for Superman* illustrates just how much
pent up demand for good schools there is.

For donors designing an education strategy, good charter schools will often be
centerpieces to be studied, supported, and expanded. Vehicles such as the Charter
School Growth Fund and the NewSchools Venture Fund now provide donors
with an efficient way to replicate high-performing charter schools that have prov-
en they can take children from disadvantaged backgrounds and graduate them
from high school and send them to college at high rates. The KIPP schools—
numbering 125 elementary, middle, and high schools nationwide as of late 2012,
serving 41,000 students—enroll 95 percent African-American and Latino students, 87 percent of whom qualify by income for free or reduced-price school
lunch. Yet more than 80 percent go on to college.[9] To cite another example among
many, some 96 percent of graduates of Summit Public Schools in California (featured in *Waiting for Superman*) are accepted to a four-year college.[10]

What's fascinating about high-performing charter schools, though, and what is
a bit troubling from a broader education-reform perspective, is that many of these
high-school graduates still don't post particularly high standardized test scores or
college completion rates. KIPP recently discovered that while the vast majority of
its graduates were enrolling in college, only a third graduated within six years. That's
much better than the percentage of disadvantaged children at large, but it's lower
than KIPP would like—and it's one reason schools in the network have been looking at blended learning and its potential for boosting rigor and deepening actual
intellectual attainment.

Another troubling question is how widely high-performing charter
schools can expand. Sometimes the business model is not sustainable on state

8. Stanford University, Center for Research on Education Outcomes, *Multiple Choice: Charter School Performance in 16 States*, 2009, http://credo.stanford.edu/reports/MULTIPLE_CHOICE_CREDO.pdf.

9. KIPP Foundation, *The Promise of College Completion: KIPP's Early Successes and Challenges; Executive Summary*, April 28, 2011, http://www.kipp.org/files/dmfile/ExecutiveSummary.pdf.

10. Summit Public Schools, 2013, http://www.summitps.org/.

per-pupil allocations. Charter schools typically receive much lower total reimbursements from states than traditional public schools. As a result, many rely on philanthropy and grassroots fundraising to stay afloat. This is yet another place where blended learning may be able to reinforce and magnify the value of charter schools.

In addition, some successful schools lean heavily on exceptional individuals who cannot be cloned—a principal willing to work 70-hour weeks, for instance, who inspires her teachers do the same. Brian Greenberg, CEO of the Silicon Schools Fund, a nonprofit fund that supports the creation of new blended-learning schools, notes that many high-performing charters "aren't scalable under the old model—because you don't have enough great teachers. It burns people out." He spent 12 years in schools, and "I lasted four times longer than most."

School choice is rooted in the same facts of competition that hone the rest of our economy.

While some people accuse charter schools of skimming up the cream of high-performing students, studies have show that to be wholly inaccurate. It may be true, however, as Greenberg notes, that because of their flexible administration and high standards, charter schools skim up "the best teachers, not kids. There are not enough of these people to go around."

A wonderful charter school can help hundreds and eventually thousands of students, making it a worthy recipient of charity of all sorts. But where philanthropy is undertaken with the goal of changing education broadly, saving one neighborhood of children is a miracle with limits. While they are growing fast, charter schools are still only 6 percent of all schools today. For many donors, wider scale is the goal.

Ambitious donors want to take a charter school that works and make 100 more just like it. Ideally they'd like these schools to operate without requiring any extra funding beyond the per-pupil financial allocations for charter schools that are provided by each state (which are often unfairly set well below the allocations for conventional schools). If blended learning can help address these sorts of practicalities—by stretching the supply of good teachers, by providing proven standardized curricula, by reducing operating costs to the level of state reimbursements—then it becomes much more likely that America's millions of poorly educated children can get schooling that draws them closer to their potential.

Accountability

The second front in the larger battle for education reform is accountability, and here too blended learning may prove a powerful tool. Accountability, mostly in the form of testing, was the backbone of No Child Left Behind, President George W. Bush's 2003 law that mandated annual testing in grades 3–8 in reading and math. The law required schools to show adequate yearly progress toward a goal of having all students proficient in reading and math by 2014. Schools that consistently failed to show progress could be shut down.

The No Child Left Behind law was a blunt instrument. It did make accountability, and the tracking of student data, part of the national conversation, and that was a huge advance. Few people now argue that students shouldn't be tested. Only holdouts believe that you can't tell anything about a school or a teacher from the test results of students (subscribing to the defeatist attitude that Newark school superintendent Cami Anderson describes as "I taught it; they didn't learn it.") But there were big problems with NCLB, too.

In deference to federalism, states were allowed to create their own NCLB tests and competency thresholds. Some watered them down to the point that passing had little or nothing to do with mastery of the subject. The National Center for Education Statistics has, for years, benchmarked state proficiency standards against the National Assessment of Educational Progress—a uniform, national assessment sometimes called "the nation's report card."[11] In 2009, achieving a proficient score in eighth-grade math on Alabama's state assessment corresponded with a 246 on the NAEP. In Massachusetts, the proficiency standard corresponded with a 300. Even if Alabama and Massachusetts showed similar pass rates, students in Alabama would be much less prepared for college and careers.

Some critics claim a focus on testing math and reading skills has turned attention away from history, science, and the arts. And amid the pressure to get failing students up above the bar, gifted students have been neglected; a 2008 Fordham Institute report, *High-Achieving Students in the Era of No Child Left Behind*, found that progress among the top 10 percent of students has slowed compared to others.[12] One way to reduce the achievement gap, it turns out, is to lower the ceiling, rather than raise the floor.

---

11. U.S. Department of Education, Institute of Education Sciences, "Mapping State Proficiency Standards onto the NAEP Scales: Variation and Change in State Standards for Reading and Mathematics," *National Assessment of Educational Progress*, (2009), http://nces.ed.gov/nationsreportcard/pdf/studies/2011458.pdf.

12. Steve Farkas, Ann Duffett, and Tom Loveless, *High-Achieving Students in the Era of No Child Left Behind*, Fordham Institute, June 18, 2008, http://208.106.213.194/detail/news.cfm?news_id=732&id=.

What Can Blended-learning Advocates Learn from Charter School Creation?

"With the benefit of hindsight, the charter school movement would have fared a lot better if, from the outset, it had paid far more attention to the quality and effectiveness of these new schools, not just their numbers; to both sides of the 'charter bargain' (i.e. both freedom and accountability); and to the new-fangled governance arrangement that we know as 'authorizing.'

"The partisans of digital and blended learning—and I count myself as one of them—need to avoid similar mistakes, which is to say they need to think much more comprehensively about what's needed for their idea to be effective, efficient and uncompromised—not just to spread across the land."

—Chester Finn Jr., president, Thomas B. Fordham Foundation

The education establishment is shuffling and stumbling beyond NCLB. The majority of states have now been granted exemptions to meeting the law's standards. Education reformers have been working on the problems that block true accountability in teaching.

Most intriguingly, under powerful leadership from the Bill & Melinda Gates Foundation and other private philanthropists, 45 states have signed on to the idea of a "Common Core"—a series of rigorous objectives that all students should know to be college and career ready, and which all these states would agree to test. The mission statement of the Common Core standards is that they will "provide a consistent, clear understanding of what students are expected to learn, so teachers and parents know what they need to do to help them. The standards are designed to be robust and relevant to the real world, reflecting the knowledge and skills that our young people need for success in college and careers. With American students fully prepared for the future, our communities will be best positioned to compete successfully in the global economy."[13]

---

13. Common Core State Standards Initiative, "Mission Statement," 2012, http://www.corestandards.org.

The Common Core—and basing annual tests on the objectives spelled out within it—is an exciting idea. But annual tests are just too slow, infrequent, impersonal, and inexact to be adequate in the digital era. Even individual quizzes or papers—the way many teachers assess what each of their students know and don't—are needlessly slow and laborious and often fail to produce useable results. Say you get a 70 percent on a math test. What does that mean? You got a "C" and hence you passed, and the class is moving forward, but a 70 means you don't know almost a third of the tested material. What if that 30 percent is critical to a later learning objective? Do you have a chance to go back and try again and learn from what you got wrong?

To address this problem, many textbooks circle back to earlier material in their first chapters, but this is a blunt instrument too. Kids who have mastered the earlier material get needlessly bored and waste time when it's presented again. And for kids who didn't get it the first time, presenting it again the same way may not help, any more than speaking English louder will increase comprehension for someone who speaks Chinese.

The testing needed to assess whether students are actually catching on can also overload teachers. Grading tests, worksheets, and papers is numbingly tedious. Moreover, test results can be hard to draw conclusions from, since most classes clump together students with a wide mix of abilities. What do you do as a teacher if you can see that 20 percent of the class knows the material cold, 50 percent can sometimes produce the right answer, and 30 percent of the class is completely confused? Even if you have this data, you can do little with it given your need to teach this highly mixed group as a group, without much time for individual tailoring.

Blended-learning classrooms don't just allow more finely screened assessment. They also provide more individualized opportunities to respond to the specific deficiencies of each student. The computerized assessment mechanism is yoked directly to a computerized instruction mechanism that can immediately be used to fill in the gaps in understanding that have been uncovered.

To think about how outdated old-style group teaching can be, contrast annual testing, or even regular in-class tests, to another thing students spend a lot of time on: video games. The "levels" in video games are an immediate personalized adaptation to where each player stands in knowledge and competence. You move up only after you master the level where you start. You can't advance if you're 70 percent through the obstacle course, or 70 percent of the way to rescuing the princess. When you've beaten a level, you know it.

In their video games, students don't have to wait a week or a month for a single test to find out if they've mastered the skills necessary to move forward to the next

Slow Uptake of Technology in Both Health Care and Education

Education isn't the only field that's been slow to adopt improved ways of doing things via technological breakthroughs. People joke about doctors' handwriting, but it has taken years of pressure from insurers and government for medical practices to adopt even today's rudimentary electronic medical records. Without easy access to a patient's medical history, healthcare workers order repeated and unnecessary tests or don't learn from treatment protocols tried before. This is very like teachers who lack easy access to a student's education history (best created from numerous micro-assessments, not one blunt end-of-year test) and thus waste weeks, if not months, of the school year figuring out where everyone stands.

The healthcare field is also just starting to unite behind evidence-based medicine, which involves following certain tested protocols after an initial diagnosis. There's a case to be made for evidence-based teaching, too. A teacher who encounters a child who is two grade levels behind in math but closer to grade level in reading may have tricks up her sleeve to help, but she seldom knows what tools have been proven to work in the past for students with similar profiles. If she had clear evidence in front of her, she could be far more effective in bringing that child up to grade level.

Why are education and health care so resistant to technological refurbishment? One explanation is that both establishments have the government as their dominant customer. Both sectors rely heavily on funding from the government which sets rules and rates in monopolistic ways, without the competition that constantly refreshes other industries.

level. The feedback is instant on each skill. They get usable data in real time. Kids tend to choose games that are just a little bit more difficult than what they're comfortable with, so they're reasonably challenged, yet able to succeed with hard work. Frequent practice combined with constant feedback leads to mastery. That is the potentially revolutionary innovation that, at least in theory, separates tech-assisted learning from earlier forms of education.

Smart games collect mind-boggling volumes of data; DreamBox, the popular math software program for elementary-school students, records 50,000 data points per student per hour.[14] Technology can do amazing things with information, not only in games but in everything it touches. Consider a retail store trying to figure out what to stock. "Can you imagine Wal-Mart operating without point-of-sale data?" asks John Danner, founder of the Rocketship schools, one of the early explorers of blended education. The stores wouldn't make it through a week, because their rock-bottom prices depend on accurate prediction of what customers have, need, and want.

Immediate, specific, personalized data can transform education as thoroughly as it has transformed retailing, our phone system, and hundreds of other sectors—leading to lower costs, more individual service and customization, and better outcomes. It can enable mastery learning, when students move at their own pace as they demonstrate knowledge, rather than at whatever pace the syllabus dictates. Technology could revolutionize teaching.

> Good blended-learning software measures progress by placing final results in the context of where a student began.

It's amazing, though, how little it has transformed to date. There has been no great technology ripple in schooling, as there has been in almost every other sector of America within the last generation. The tendency in schools has simply been to layer technology lightly on top of existing practices, without fundamentally changing anything. Some new devices have been bolted onto the 1950s model of a classroom, but there has been little rethinking of fundamentals. "We've taken for granted that school has to be a teacher standing at the front of a box filled with 25 kids," states Alex Hernandez, partner at the Charter School Growth Fund. "When you loosen that constraint, what can school look like?"

This is where new-style digital learning may be a game-changer. If computerized curricula that include constant student testing become widespread in classrooms, with daily reports showing how every student in a class is doing on various fronts, then accountability becomes much

---

14. Jessie Woolley-Wilson (CEO, DreamBox Learning), in discussion with author.

easier to enforce. Teachers, principals, and parents will know right away if students are learning and understanding.

Good blended-learning software puts all final results in the context of where the student started out, so separating good instruction from bad instruction isn't just a crude matter of who aces the end-of-year test. What each class adds to the pre-existing stock of skills of each child within it becomes the measuring stick. That is fairer to teachers working with difficult students, and it prevents complacency among teachers fortunate to start a year with high-achieving students. This focus on individual results opens new options to donors who insist that their investments should make demonstrable differences in children's lives.

What Does Blended Learning Look Like in Practice?

New blended learning programs are beginning to be spawned in many parts of the U. S. Some early-adopting charter schools have already gone through a few academic years testing different approaches to blended learning. In many cases these schools have been energized by philanthropic dollars as they've pursued their objectives, studied what works, and gradually expanded. Their experiences offer insights that other foundations wanting to invest in this field need to know about.

In addition to its operative contributions, the philanthropic community has also played a major role in bringing public attention to these blended-learning pathbreakers, so that other educators, policy makers, and families can know what options exist. The Jaquelin Hume Foundation, for instance, has supported the creation of several promotional videos on blended-learning schools (see sidebar on page 39). In 2011, the Michael & Susan Dell Foundation commissioned white-paper studies of five blended learning schools— Rocketship, Summit, College-ready Public Schools, KIPP Los Angeles, and the FirstLine schools in New Orleans. These in-depth profiles probe the finances and instruction and operation models of all of these schools (you can find links to them in the appendix). "We wanted to tell a very rich story about what it means to look at and understand and potentially operate models like these," says Cheryl Niehaus, an education program officer at the Dell Foundation.

When it comes to blended learning, seeing is believing. In that spirit, here are quick profiles of some of the best-known blended-learning schools.

Rocketship Education

Before co-founding Rocketship Education in 2006 (with Preston Smith), John Danner had two careers: as a Silicon Valley CEO whose start-up, NetGravity, was acquired in a 1999 stock deal valued at $530 million, and as an educator in Nashville. He brought experiences from both these ventures to Rocketship—perhaps the best-known of the blended-learning school models. Rocketship focuses primarily on low-income and urban students, and requires fewer teachers than traditional school models, yet still achieves better results.

Rocketship's first school opened in San Jose, California, in 2007. Mateo Sheedy Elementary School serves about 500 students, 88 percent of whom qualify for free or reduced-price lunch, and 65 percent of whom are learning English as a second language. Danner and his team subsequently opened six more elementary schools in the San Jose area, and (with funding from the Lynde and Harry Bradley Foundation) plan to expand to Milwaukee in the fall of 2013. The organization has also won charters to operate in New Orleans, Indianapolis, Memphis, Nashville, and Washington, D.C. The ultimate goal is to operate in 50 cities and serve one million children. Though a number of foundations have aided Rocketship's growth, key aspects of the organization's business model make day-to-day operations and replication financially sustainable in a way few other charter schools have been able to emulate.

Here's what a Rocketship education looks like. On a balmy California May day, parent volunteers with younger kids in tow are humming around the school receptionist at Rocketship Mosaic Elementary, located on Owsley Avenue in San Jose. Most of the students and parents are Hispanic (English is a second language for 80 percent of the students at this location). Signs on the wall honor the parents who've put in the most volunteer hours. Some reach the "Jupiter" level—500–600 hours—by May. That's the equivalent of a serious part-time job.

The building is bright, clean, and cheery. Some kids play outside, others sit in classrooms—very typical, colorful elementary school classrooms that are not technology-based at all. The only noticeably distinguishing feature of the school is a large Learning Lab set up in what would be the cafeteria in many schools. Since this is sunny California, children here eat lunch outside on picnic tables under a green awning, munching on Revolution Foods (a provider of healthy fare).

In the Learning Lab, dozens of children sit at Acer computers ($150 apiece) in long rows, separated by brightly painted cardboard dividers. Students cycle through this lab, spending approximately two hours per day

> By educating students for about 15 percent less than the normal state allotment, Rocketship's business model makes replication financially sustainable— unlike many other charter schools.

there. The software—games and problem sets from different providers—runs about $20 per student in group licenses, and since it's not bandwidth-gulping video, a basic Comcast broadband package suffices to power the lab. When the children shuffle in, they sit down and follow signs reminding them of the proper learning posture: headphones on, no talking, raise your hand if you need help.

The software covers basic elementary-school skills: reading and math. But each child is covering a different set of skills at any given time. Every child's sequence of programs, sometimes called a "playlist," is a little different. Over the years, Rocketship's educators have developed algorithms to predict which programs different kinds of students will respond best to. If you're an English-language learner with certain test scores, for instance, you'll get one default playlist, to be changed as needed. Teachers get immediate data on how students are doing on different skills. During the rest of the day when the kids are not on the computers, they receive small-group instruction from teachers informed by computerized data, and do group projects.

In 2013, Rocketship announced they would be modifying their Learning Labs, placing three teachers with each pod of 90 students in the lab, and integrating more direct instruction with the online resources. Children will still cycle through work at the screen and keyboard using their individual playlist, but it will happen closer to their teacher, with the hope of gaining closer integration between what the machine offers and how the teacher follows up.

The two hours per day of computer instruction will still allow teachers to avoid burning time teaching or reviewing basic concepts that machines do better. "It's insane that most schools do spelling in classrooms," says Danner. There are many opportunities to teach children repetitive, drill-intensive tasks like this more effectively by computer. The teacher can focus sticking points with students individually or in small groups.

As Rocketship alters its Learning Labs, it will be crucial to see if they can maintain what has been one of their biggest comparative advantages to this point: the boost in teacher productivity that comes from reserving teachers for higher-level instruction, while using aides to oversee children's time at the computer stations.

The Learning Lab model allowed Rocketship to operate with roughly six fewer teachers per school, meaning that "we save 25 percent of salary costs," says Danner. "When you have that, you can grow without raising additional capital." Even after paying its smaller number of teachers better than other schools, Rocketship is able to educate a child for about 15 percent less than California's annual per-pupil allotment, and it plows that margin of funds into, among other things, teacher training and opening new schools. Hence, the model should be able to expand like successful businesses do, without constantly needing new financial angels or capital infusions.

"True blended schools," says Danner, "are financially scalable." Rocketship itself is in the midst of rapid growth. It has plans to expand from seven schools to more than 20 over the next five years.

More important than the cost savings, though, is that Rocketship's financially attractive model gets results:

- The network had an overall score of 855 on the 2012 California Academic Performance Index (API). The target for schools is 800.

- Even though 90 percent of their students are low income, and 70 percent come from non-English-speaking homes, fully 80 percent of Rocketship students scored at the "proficient" or "advanced" level for math on the California Standards Test—not far from the 83 percent of students in California's 10 most affluent districts who scored the same.

Of course, there are other things besides the blended-learning model driving results at Rocketship schools. The culture of parent involvement matters a great deal. If kids see their mothers and fathers in the school building frequently—and 500-600 hours over 30 weeks would count as frequently—they'll get the message that learning is important.

Rocketship also has many excellent teachers. Danner exaggerates only a little when he says he has pretty much outsourced his teacher recruiting to Teach For America. He takes a number of TFA placements each year, and also hires alums of the program. While TFA members are younger and don't have much experience, many of them come from top colleges, and its recruitment process is quite selective. More than 48,000 young people applied for about 5,800 TFA placements in 2012.

And Rocketship's teachers are not unionized. The lack of union restrictions lets the schools adapt quickly and transform themselves as conditions demand. Rocketship also pays teachers more—at least 15 percent more, and up to 30 percent more than neighboring district teachers.[1]

Rocketship has worked through plenty of challenges over the past few years, and will face more as it expands. For instance: student playlists often include software from multiple providers, in order to capture the best approach to each topic. But the software doesn't integrate easily. As the Dell report on Rocketship noted:

There is no common definition of mastery across online programs. This means, for example, that when one program reports that a student has mastered fractions, this conclusion may not be shared by other online programs or by Rocketship's own system of classroom assessments. Taken together, these issues mean that it has been difficult for Rocketship teachers to access the sort of consistent and reliable data on student progress towards the mastery of standards that they would use to directly drive classroom instruction. Instead, the data that teachers currently access is most useful for showing which students are on task, which can be helpful in motivating students and managing student behavior.

---

1. See, for example, "Can Rocketship Launch a Fleet of Successful, Mass-Produced Schools?" *PBS Newshour*, December 28, 2012, http://www.pbs.org/newshour/bb/education/july-dec12/ rocket_12-28.html.

First Lady of Digital Education

No one has done more to take blended learning from obscure concept to national movement than Gisèle Huff, the executive director (and lone employee) of the Jaquelin Hume Foundation, a small San Francisco–based philanthropy whose grants have had outsized impact.

"Education has always been a very important part of my life," Huff says. She and her mother came to the U.S. from France after World War II with "$400 to our names, the clothes on our backs and in our suitcases. We didn't speak any English." The American education system made it possible for her to earn a Ph.D., have a business career, teach, and even run for Congress. She wants other children to have those same opportunities. That's why her first years at the Hume Foundation were spent advancing school choice. But as she points out, "we were in the business of school choice for 10 years and we had bloody foreheads to show for it." She came to the idea of digital learning after hearing Clayton Christensen speak in 2005. She loved the idea that technology could transform, not reform, education.

The Hume Foundation's first digital-learning grant was $50,000 to the Innosight Institute, in part to support the writing and promotion of *Disrupting Class.* "I saw that as a seminal book and a seminal idea, and that's what it turned out to be," Huff says. To advance thinking about digital education, she also gave an early grant to iNACOL.

As educational entrepreneurs began starting blended learning schools, the Hume Foundation made grants for public relations tasks: $100,000 to Rocketship, $100,000 to Carpe Diem. These grants paid for videos that helped people see what blended learning looks like, and were successful to the point that Carpe Diem founder Rick Ogston was soon a major figure in a one-hour Juan Williams television special. (When Huff met Ogston and heard what he was up to, she reports that she told him "hold on to your hat—people are going to know about you.") Rocketship has been profiled in *USA Today* and other publications. "It's unbelievable what $100,000 did," says Huff. Her foundation has also paid for journalist-education days that introduce influential writers to the concept of blended learning.

Hume Foundation money, along with grants from the Harry Singer Foundation and some individual donors, also established The Learning Accelerator. This group hopes to organize the investment of $100 million of philanthropic and commercial money to help blended-learning service providers set up operations in school districts across the country. In 2013 the group received its first substantial infusion of capital, a $750,000 grant from the Gates Foundation.

As money from other foundations has followed Hume's giving, Huff now reports that "I'm out of charter schools. Now we're doing districts." Painting on this larger canvas is the next way the Hume Foundation's risk-taking strategy could lead other funders. But even as the kinds of schools the foundation supports have changed, the organization is all-in on digital learning. "We gave up everything else," says Huff. Arguments about teacher evaluations and merit pay and school choice remind her of reports that cities commissioned around the turn of the 20th century on what to do about the burgeoning problem of horse excrement soiling the streets. With rising populations, everyone assumed it would get worse. "A friend tells me that one proposed solution was to put diapers on the horses," says Huff, laughing. "Meanwhile, Henry Ford was just around the corner. This is exactly what's happening now. The reformers are putting diapers on horses. Yet digital learning is just around the corner."

Rocketship has elected to store its software in the cloud whenever possible to save money on IT infrastructure. But, as in all blended-learning programs, IT needs are more intense than in traditional schools.

The quality of the software content isn't always great, though it's getting better. One of the biggest problems the school has faced is that the six different major programs they use all have different mechanisms for measuring results and giving teachers feedback. Sometimes that's too cumbersome to help teachers know what they need to explain differently the next day.[2]

_____

2. For a discussion of some of the things the school is seeking to improve, see previous footnote.

Nonetheless, Danner is optimistic about solving blended-learning headaches as they come up. He has turned to philanthropists for help in the early stages of development and expansion before the benefits of scale are achieved. The Gates Foundation, for instance, paid for a program that helps integrate different software so children can use a single sign-on and teachers can have more useable data. This program will be useful for other schools adopting blended models as well.

With this assistance, Rocketship Education has refined its model over time so that it is more easily duplicated. "We've seen our peaks and valleys flatten over the last five years," says Danner. "Now when we're opening a new school, 50 percent of the result is almost guaranteed unless someone sets fire to the computers. Most schools don't have that cushion."

To capitalize on the valuable experience Rocketship is gaining, the Hume Foundation gave a $100,000 grant to the school to pay for public relations and bringing John Danner to speak at different events. This helped raise the profile of Rocketship nationally. The Eli and Edythe Broad Foundation invested $1 million, starting in 2010, to support Rocketship's growth and expansion over a three-year period.

Alliance Technology and Math-science High School (ATAMS)

Alliance Technology and Math-Science students use the in-class rotation model. ATAMS is one of five high schools housed at the Sonia M. Sotomayor campus in Los Angeles. This brand new complex was built to ease overcrowding, and much of it is shiny and new, with an inspiring view of the mountains from the open-air common areas.

All ATAMS students have gleaming white Apple laptops, and in each large classroom students are broken into three groups doing different things. Some are progressing solo through individual problem sets on their laptops. Others are working on group projects. The rest are working with the teacher. They cycle through these three stations in each class.

The most striking thing about ATAMS classes is how many students are in each group: 16. This gives each ATAMS class an official student-to-teacher ratio of 48:1. Yet with students absorbed in their laptops, the classes feel surprisingly intimate and engaged. Moving between three stations in each class period means it "doesn't get as boring," says Paulina, a student. "You get to switch around. For me, it makes the time go quicker."

Those teacher ratios create vital economic advantages for ATAMS. The combination of salary efficiencies and careful control of online content costs should ultimately allow each of the schools to save more than $1 million over five years, compared to a conventional school, even including startup costs. That encourages donors to think the model can economically spread to many places.

The material that students cover each day in an ATAMS classroom is partially differentiated for each individual. A glance around laptops in an English class, for instance, finds that everyone is reading about the USDA's different climate zones. But students report that some of the reading passages have more advanced vocabulary than others, depending on how much a student shows he or she can handle.

Teachers get immediate data on how their students are doing—which the students pick up on. "The teachers are more on you," says Chauncey, a young man who shows the dashboard on his laptop to a group of visitors tiptoeing through his class. "They know you more. They care about how you're doing." Students can see instantly how they're doing too, he says, so they understand what they have to work on. Mickie Tubbs, the school's principal, agrees: "That's the magic of this model. It's personal."

There are kinks still being worked out in achieving this ideal of personalized education. Partial differentiation is better than no differentiation, but differentiation in ATAMS classes still occurs within a relatively narrow band. This is partly a function of the available software—something all blended-learning schools are struggling with as educators try to bridge the gap between the leading edge of adaptive software and daily classroom realities—and partially a function of sticking very closely to a three-station rotational model. The ATAMS staff is quite enthusiastic about this model, and though it does make classes go quickly, the downside is that it serves to keep the whole class on fairly similar material. After all, every subject must include group-project time, whether that group work is producing obvious benefits or not.

This portion of the ATAMS formula is the least proven. The case study on ATAMS produced by the Dell Foundation found that "staff have acknowledged that the collaborative station might lack this element of rigor . . . whereas the direct and online settings foster rigorous instruction on state standards." Steps to rectify this include giving students specific roles in the group rotation, letting them rate themselves and each other, and offering exit slips from this station. Whether that's enough is not clear. "Collaboration" is a perennially popular cause among educators, but making it (and related strategies like "peer tutoring") work in practice is difficult, whether you're in a blended school or not, and it's possible that hewing to a three-station model will prevent break-

Changing an Obsolete System

Like Gisèle Huff and the Hume Foundation, Frank Baxter had scars from years of trying to improve education. "I've been involved in school reform since 1986," says Baxter. His career also includes a 13-year period as CEO of investment bank Jefferies & Company, and a stint as President George W. Bush's Ambassador to Uruguay.

In addition to acting as a donor himself, Baxter became co-chairman of the board of the Alliance College-ready Public Schools, a high-performing charter network launched in 2004 that expanded rapidly and graduated virtually all its students. Yet despite those successes, "it occurred to me that what we were doing was making the best of an obsolete system." The campaigners who created the American public school system in the mid-1800s were "trying to prepare our pastoral, illiterate nation for the Industrial Revolution," says Baxter. Their invention "functioned pretty well up to the middle of the 20th century." But the world has changed since then.

The economy now values independent thought, not uniformity. Meanwhile, as the world demanded more of teachers, quality declined, since our old schools were built "on the availability of qualified women who had to work at a fraction of what they can get elsewhere today." Reform efforts produced all kinds of responses. "Many of the ideas were really good from a management standpoint: more accountability, more training, more pay. That's business 101. But nothing happened," says Baxter.

People blamed just about everyone: "The teachers are no good. The kids are no good. The parents are no good." But what, asks Baxter, if most people are doing their best, but "there's something wrong with the model?"

That question, plus Baxter's long-standing interest in technology ("I always think, 'never send a person to do a machine's job'") led him to support blended-learning pilots in the Alliance schools, like the one described in this guidebook's profile of the Alliance Technology and Math-science High School (ATAMS). The fact that they were running charters, not traditional public schools, allowed for the possibility of innovation. "We've had the luxury of being more outcome-oriented," he says.

As his teams now study the outcomes, "I'm totally convinced that it works. There's still not enough data to really verify that." But students and teachers are excited about learning in a way he hasn't seen before. "It just clearly is a better system," he says. "It's scalable, it's rapidly improving, and it's sustainable."

Recently, Baxter has been having conversations with the Los Angeles Unified School District (LAUSD)

on expanding blended-learning more broadly across the city. "I was worried, because there'd be a threat of reducing the number of teachers," he says. But he learned that due to enrollment and budget problems the LAUSD already had over 40 students in the classroom in some places, without the balancing advantages of blended-learning stations. In those stressed schools, "blended learning is going to be very attractive to them."

throughs that might otherwise result from the strengths of the online and small-group instruction.

Despite these challenges, something in the ATAMS method is powerful. In one academic year, the first cohort of mostly minority, high-poverty students achieved multiple years of academic gains, according to Frank Baxter, co-chairman of ATAMS' umbrella organization. This brought the achievement average for the students enrolled from way below grade level up to something approaching the norm. Behavior is also much better. Students become engaged in their own progress and "there are no disciplinary problems," says Baxter. "I walk in pretty frequently and very few heads come up. They're so involved in what they're doing."

Tubbs notes that the ability of this more personalized teaching method to meet students at approximately their level means that teachers feel less burdened by their lagging students—students who the data reveal have been woefully underserved by their primary schools. Wendy Chaves, who teaches math at ATAMS, says that "a lot of kids need remediation. They have a lot of learning gaps." She discovered that "sophomores didn't know how to do fractions. It's difficult to learn algebra II when you don't have those concepts." She's spent much time trying to encourage students who "hated math, flunked math. Everything they tried did not work out." But as they take charge of their own learning, she's trying "to mold them and have them see their potential. I want to make them aware that they do have potential, they just haven't had a chance to succeed."

Tubbs agrees that at teacher meetings "the conversation isn't about 'that kid.' It's about 'how can you help me solve this problem with this kid?'"This new interest in appropriate instruction—rather than mass teaching that tries to pound a uniform curriculum into varied students all at the same pace—should pay dividends in the long run. Based on experience at its blended-learning schools, the Alliance for College-Ready Public Schools (of which ATAMS is a part) is adopting blended models in the new schools it opens. The Broad Foundation is helping to fund this expansion with start-up capital so the schools can plan and purchase technology. The Hume Foundation also gave a grant of $100,000 to help ATAMS with a curious logistical problem: based on initial positive results, the school has so many visitors and queries that it needs additional staff just to handle these requests.

Summit Rainier and Tahoma

Diane Tavenner worked as a public-school teacher and administrator for a decade before founding Summit Public Schools, a network of charter schools in the San Francisco Bay area. Summit schools aim to make all students college ready. The

> The personalized teaching made possible by new technology allows teachers to meet students at their level.

network hires high-quality teachers and provides them with 40 days of professional training every year. Students get insights into careers and non-traditional subjects through a four-week intersession, during which they can take courses on anything from dance to professional cooking.

At Summit schools, all kids take multiple Advanced Placement classes. Almost all graduates (96 percent) are accepted at four-year colleges. Yet, according to spokeswoman Mira Browne, when Summit's leadership team looked at the first graduates' performance in college, they realized that many had needed remedial classes, particularly in math, and many others had not persisted to graduation. Roughly half graduated from college on schedule.

"That's still triple the national average," Browne says, "but for us at Summit it's not nearly good enough. That's not why we're here. We want 100 percent into college, through college, and becoming contributing members of the workforce and society."

School leaders realized that even as they successfully taught each year's curriculum, their students had unfilled gaps from earlier in their schooling. While "our kids are taking and passing AP Calculus . . . what we weren't able to do in the current model is fill in every single one of the holes and gaps from elementary school." So they turned to blended learning to make sure students mastered basic skills before they took up later subjects.

In 2011 the Summit network opened two new schools called Summit Rainier and Summit Tahoma, housed in the same campus near National Hispanic University in San Jose. These schools began using blended learning in math courses, based primarily on the Khan Academy's free library of online videos with math problem sets. A team from the Khan Academy (whose staffing was made possible, in part, by grants from the Gates Foundation) worked directly with Summit teachers to make the math sequences work for students in a classroom environment, and to give teachers useful feedback via a "coach" feature that allows a teacher or parent to log into a dashboard and check on student progress.

The schools were sufficiently happy with the results from 2011–2012 that teachers made plans to use more blended learning during the 2012–2013 school year, and to expand the use of blended learning within Summit's charter management organization, an undertaking funded in part by a $2 million investment from the Charter School Growth Fund. Much of this curriculum development was worked out during the Summit schools' annual 40 days of professional development. One thing teachers talked about a lot during this time was how to use blended learning to meet the needs of the top 10 percent and the bottom 10 percent of students—populations that get lost in the shuffle under mass teaching methods. In theory, blended learning should easily meet these students' needs, yet they proved slightly more difficult to serve in Summit's model than theory would suggest.

"We felt like we did a really good job opening up the class in a way that students could work at things at their own pace—and not get rushed if they

Even students who successfully learn the year's curriculum sometimes have unfilled gaps from earlier in their schooling. Blended learning is able to find and fill these.

Sal Khan and Serendipitous Philanthropy

Sal Khan famously began filming his narrated math videos in his closet in 2004. By 2009 he and a handful of educators had launched programs using Khan Academy in a few schools. Several thousand students were watching the videos and working through his problem sets every day. "I was spending every ounce of my free time to work on it," he writes in his 2012 book, *The One World Schoolhouse*. "Actually I was even spending a little of my nonfree time," he says, and so in late summer 2009 he decided to quit his job at a hedge fund and give himself a year to make Khan Academy work.

A few months into the experiment, he was stressed out and burning through $5,000 a month to support his family. But in April, he received an unsolicited $10,000 donation from Ann Doerr, wife of the famous venture capitalist John Doerr. A friend's child had been helped by Khan Academy videos and she was intrigued. She and Khan met for lunch; she later gave him $100,000 to stay afloat. Two months after that meeting, she sent him a text message that Bill Gates was mentioning him in a speech at the Aspen Ideas Festival. Gates turned out to be using Khan Academy videos to brush up on his own math skills and to help his children.

And so a year after quitting his hedge fund job, Sal Khan was in Gates' offices in Kirkland, Washington, answering questions. The Gates Foundation soon invested $1.5 million in Khan Academy for operations and then later gave another $4 million for other projects. Google awarded $2 million to build out the problem sets and translate content into ten languages. Khan Academy is now being used in numerous schools, including the high-performing Los Altos School District, and in the Summit Public Schools profiled in this guidebook.

While philanthropists often devise a strategy and then look to fund people working in that area, the funding of the Khan Academy has been more about the serendipity of stumbling upon an excellent service or product and then investing in what you have grown to admire. "The Gates Foundation didn't come at it from a traditional angle—some thesis that we want to be sponsoring open education resources and find a scalable model," says Khan in an interview. "They kind of just bumped into me. They were using it. Bill Gates was using Khan Academy with his kids. A lot of folks at Google were using it for their kids and themselves." These funders realized, "I've gotten value out of this. It would be a shame if other people wouldn't get it because this guy can't pay his bills."

Khan thinks of this as more like a venture-capital mindset: investing in something you find impressive. He argues that philanthropists should do more to encourage entrepreneurship in the nonprofit sector. There are lots of people willing to launch experiments for very little money in order to have a shot at the kind of validation that comes from creating something new and effective and beloved. That kind of energy can be harnessed in the nonprofit sector just as it is in for-profit work, Khan believes.

To be sure, for-profit start-ups hope for big payoffs down the road when they go public or get acquired. Working for a nonprofit start-up is "not as much of a lottery ticket," Khan says. So "you'd probably have to pay a little better." Thanks to philanthropy money, at Khan Academy, people make "upper quartile Silicon Valley pay," and that enables Khan to answer in the affirmative the question: "Are we getting the very best talent, not a subset of talent that's just willing to sacrifice a lot?"

Yet money isn't everything. "I'm meeting a lot of entrepreneurs who are looking to do the next cool thing," says Khan. "They're looking to have the next big impact. They care about money because it gives you certain abilities to do things. But they're not in it to drive a Ferrari one day. Their pride is 'I changed an industry.'"

So what would have happened to Khan Academy if Doerr, Gates, and Google hadn't come along? What was his back-up business model? "Advertising," he says. Based on page views in 2009–2010, Khan Academy could have pulled in at least $70,000–$80,000 per year in ads. "That definitely would have allowed me to survive, but it would have been unfortunate," says Khan. "It would have become very commercial very fast." Picture 15-second ads for Coca-Cola before each trigonometry video: "That's what I would have had to do to keep making Khan Academy."

didn't understand, or not get slowed down—mostly with the middle 80 percent of students," says Jesse Roe, a Summit math teacher. But at the extremes, things were more complicated.

"Our top 10 percent could have been challenged more. A lot of the reason for that is a bandwidth issue on our part. We're always trying to create new content for those students, but we didn't have time to create something really rich. So now we're trying to improve on our top-end content. . . . We want to always have something available for students when they race ahead."

As for the 10 percent of students who were struggling most? "We completely did our best trying to allow them to go through at their own pace, and go as far back in content as needed," says Roe, but the problem was that Summit's teachers were "still expecting all students to go through the algebra

> The goal is for every child to get instruction on the material he has yet to master, regardless of where that material falls in grade status.

and geometry course." With an eye on meeting the ninth- and tenth-grade standards on time, "we probably didn't give them enough time to develop that foundation." After discussion and development, though, "We're moving toward a competency-based model, where it doesn't matter if you're in ninth or tenth grade." The goal is to create an environment where a child gets instruction on the material that he has yet to master, no matter what his grade status. Better to go back and fix knowledge gaps, because "your skipping this content and not developing a foundation will just slow down your learning in the future."

As Summit moves toward competency-based learning, it aims to focus on what students know instead of age-based grade levels. "Students work at their own pace," notes Alex Hernandez of the Charter School Growth Fund, which is supporting Summit's expansion. Eventually, students may be certified as "either high school-ready, college-ready, or career-ready."

Despite working closely with Khan Academy, there have been logistical challenges in using Khan online content as the basis for in-school classes. For instance, Khan Academy didn't have enough material to fill an entire year of class time devoted to algebra and geometry. To stay ahead of Summit's swifter students, the team writing Khan's problem sets had to race to create new and deeper extensions of subject knowledge for students achieving "streaks"—getting 10 problems in a row correct, as required to move forward under Khan Academy's mastery rubric.

Another problem was that streaming the Khan videos requires bandwidth. When 100 students watch videos simultaneously, that's a lot of bandwidth. Summit had to massively raise its technology budget in the course of the year to upgrade its internet service.

Summit has also faced architectural challenges. In a high school, where students tend to go to different classrooms for different subjects, the computers can't be in centralized learning labs—every classroom needs to be set up for blended learning. In some older school buildings like the one Summit Rainier and Tahoma inherited, a classroom might only feature two electrical outlets, let alone the high-capacity broadband necessary for video-based instruction.

These challenges are surmountable, but lining up dozens of power strips, or wheeling around a laptop-charging cart, just reinforces how different blended learning is from what most teachers and schools have dealt with before. Even experienced teachers become, in some ways, like first-year teachers, trying to keep an early-adopter mindset while still meeting the needs of the children in front of them. "This is messy stuff," says Tavenner. Like any product, "you have to test and iterate."

Carpe Diem

Carpe Diem Collegiate High School and Middle School in Yuma, Arizona, started as a traditional charter school. After losing its building lease, the school struggled to find a new space. One of the few facilities available was a former call center which featured an open floor of cubicles with offices and meeting rooms on the perimeter. School founder Rick Ogston decided to take advantage of these circumstances by shifting to a blend of heavy computer-based instruction supplemented with old-fashioned teaching.

The on-campus version of Carpe Diem (there's also a fully online version) is small—capped at 300 students in each school for grades 6–12, according to Ogston—because "we believe it's best for the culture." With 300 students, the school has a grand total of four certified teachers: one math teacher, one for science, one for social sciences, and one for language arts. That creates an official student-to-teacher ratio of 75 to 1, though there are also non-certified assistant teachers/coaches who provide instruction. Because it needs only one master instructor in each field, Carpe Diem recruits the best of the best teachers—and pays them a lot more.

Students work primarily on their computers, originally using Education2020 software (a situation that was evolving as of this guidebook's writing). There were plenty of things that weren't perfect about this software, notes Ogston, but rather than seeking out the flashiest curriculum in each subject "we prefer one that can manage the whole package for us." That gives the school better control over the whole education being offered. Ogston notes that "what we lose in flashiness we can make up in the workshops."

Those workshops are a key component of teacher interaction with students at Carpe Diem, and make the 75-to-1 student-to-teacher ratio feel relatively intimate. Teachers are "handed reports several times a day electronically." These reports inform the content of the workshops and the individualized tutoring-style instruction students receive.

This process isn't as straightforward as it sounds. "I thought that teachers initially would understand the data more," says Ogston, but he soon learned that blended learning requires a lot of professional development because the data can be "overwhelming." Teachers need to learn what is important in the scoring feedback on each child, and why, "and what do I do with it?" But after much work, "they do seem to get it," says Ogston, and it makes them more efficient. "When they are actually involved at the student-data level and know what the student needs, they don't have to spend a lot of time just shooting to the middle. They strategically go in and one-on-one with students or small groups and teach to what they need, rather than just hope to reach some people."

Another challenge? Acclimating students to self-directed learning. "Some students are not prepared for individualized learning," Ogston says. "They're used to cohort learning and not carrying their weight." Sparking motivation becomes a key job of Carpe Diem teachers—as it is in any school.

Like Rocketship, Carpe Diem offers possibilities for sustainable expansion, because it has managed to squeeze productivity gains out of technology, primarily by employing fewer teachers. This makes the school affordable, even if per-pupil allotments stagnate. Per pupil costs run about $5,000 per year. That's well below Arizona's average of $7,600 per year. These savings should allow school leaders to replicate their model broadly over time without requiring large new capital infusions.

Because it needs only one master instructor in each field, Carpe Diem school recruits the best of the best teachers.

This opens up fascinating opportunities. Dan Peters, president of the Cincinnati-based Lovett and Ruth Peters Foundation, argues that while philanthropy can incubate new school models like Carpe Diem, the most promising way to expand them into a critical mass is for them to become profitable entities that generate returns they can use to expand to the next location. "One of the main reasons progress is so slow in education reform generally is because almost all reformers are focused on the non-profit model. That means there's very limited ability to expand, since access to capital is so difficult," explains Peters.

If dramatic school improvements are going to be brought to a larger chunk of the 50 million kids now being instructed in America, the powerful tools of the profit motive need to be more widely employed, Peters argues. "K–12 is a $600 billion market," he notes. "Reformist schools don't need millions in capital, they need *billions* if they're going to reach a 5 percent market share."

As a start toward this hoped-for phase where profit margins can power continual expansion, Peters has encouraged Carpe Diem to use commercial levers to expand. His foundation provided the planning grant that allowed Carpe Diem to create its second physical school—which opened in Indianapolis in August of 2012. Then Peters helped Carpe Diem come to Cincinnati by obtaining bank loans, which will be repaid from the margin between the school's incoming fees and its costs. "If the school is as good as we're hoping, and it can retain its cost advantages, bank loans will make expansion much easier than waiting for philanthropic dollars," Peters explains. In December 2012, the Cincinnati Board of Education gave the green light to the opening of a new Carpe Diem campus in the fall of 2013.

Of course, finances are only one of the hurdles that a new-schools entrepreneur must leap. Carpe Diem's first expansion to Indianapolis was not entirely smooth. Failing to find a suitable space, Ogston had to build a new building (paid for with school start-up funds), which was completed—"dirt to fully operating school"—in 49 days. Because no one was sure if the school would open in time, some potential students enrolled elsewhere.

Local media and some bloggers also raised flags about the 75-to-1 student-to-teacher ratio. They questioned the dramatic increases of Carpe Diem students on Arizona's annual achievement tests—92 percent proficiency on the state test in 2010, as compared to 57 percent in the rest of Yuma County, and 65 percent across Arizona generally.[3] Critics questioned

---

3. Carpe Diem Schools, June 28, 2011, http://www.youtube.com/watch?v=-s_O65rWV10.

how the school could achieve such results on per-pupil costs of just over $5,000, as compared to the Arizona-wide average of $7,600, and hinted that perhaps cheating was involved.

Nonetheless, the school opened for the 2012–2013 school year. It now serves about 100 pupils from diverse backgrounds, including a number of home-schoolers used to individualized instruction but interested in coming back into the public-school fold. Ogston plans to be at the capacity of 300 students next year.

To a degree many other blended learning schools do not, Carpe Diem challenges the way people think education should look. Far from a cozy, tweedy classroom like something out of *Dead Poets Society*, Carpe Diem looks like a call center in Bangalore. Students spend big chunks of their days in cubicles. Because students conduct so much of their basic learning time on the computer, though, Ogston says this frees up time for individual face-to-face interactions on areas where they are stuck and looking for extra information. Students say "they actually get more one-on-one time with teachers here than they did in other schools."

KIPP Empower Academy

KIPP ("Knowledge Is Power Program") Public Charter Schools are already famous for their great results. The 125-member network has attracted investment from numerous philanthropies, including the Doris and Donald Fisher Fund, the Karsh Family Foundation, the Walton Family Foundation, and others. Founded in 1994 by Mike Feinberg and David Levin, KIPP schools' basic tenets are longer school days, high expectations, and character development. Some KIPP schools have been built around small class sizes, which is what Mike Kerr planned to do when he founded KIPP Empower Academy in South Central Los Angeles, a few blocks from where the riots started in 1992.

But shortly before the school opened for kindergartners in fall 2010 (it will be K–4 by 2014), California cut state spending for schools. Some other sources of funding dried up simultaneously, and suddenly Kerr was looking at class sizes of 28–30 children. The question facing the school was how to maintain small group instruction with limited finances. Blended learning promised to help with that. Kerr implemented a blended-learning model to maintain small group time with teachers, even as class sizes rose. Grants from the Riordan Foundation, funded by former Los Angeles Mayor Richard Riordan, helped KIPP purchase the additional technology necessary to implement this model.

Now, at KIPP Empower Academy, located in a few temporary classrooms within the larger Raymond Avenue School—a turquoise and tan complex of buildings, sunny courtyards, fuchsia bougainvilleas, and a very tall fence to keep the neighborhood out—classes of kindergartners rotate through three stations. In M. J. Mathis' room, nine children do math and reading problems on computers. A dozen children meet with an instructional aide, and half a dozen work with Mathis on specific issues.

The curriculum is challenging; in one kindergarten class, the children are writing stories about the rainforest in their workbooks. Some have just copied words (like "monkey") from the board, but others have written little stories in full sentences. In a first-grade class, a journal question on the wall asks, "Would you rather read a book or write a book? Why?"

KIPP Empower's classrooms are nowhere near as technology-centered as Carpe Diem's (though there have still been challenges with wiring and bandwidth—a perennial problem with opening 21st-century schools in buildings built decades prior). Students spend just 30 minutes on the computers a few times a day. The teachers can group students for in-person

> Technology applied in the right ways can transform, rather than reform, education.

instruction based on data coming out of these computer stints, though in the first years, KIPP manager Jelena Dobic reports, the data was basically useless in terms of teachers being able to quickly assess what it meant about comprehension. The school has been changing the software to close this loop, and it received a grant from the Gates Foundation to develop systems that are more user-friendly.

Even without a perfect data-feedback loop, though, and with limited computer time, results from its first school year (2010–2011) put KIPP Empower Academy at the top of new KIPP schools—something that got blended learning noticed network-wide. The L.A. institution is "a very young school, and we are always careful not to overstate," says KIPP CEO Richard Barth, but "when we look at their results both in terms of academic growth and also at other things we value—student retention, staff satisfaction, family satisfaction—they've had as good a couple of years as any elementary school we've opened." Indeed, according to KIPP network spokeswoman Zoe Fenson, KIPP Empower Academy had 100 percent staff retention from year one to year two, and one of the highest levels of teacher satisfaction across KIPP's nationwide network.

The L.A. school's results cast doubt on conventional wisdom about the supposed importance of class size. If students in 28-child classes can get better results than those in 22-child classes within the same charter network, class size can't be the most important variable. All KIPP schools have the same long school day, the same policy of allowing school leaders wide autonomy, the same strict discipline standards, and so forth. Blended learning is probably not the only variable helping KIPP Empower Academy. But it seems to be an important contribution.

School leaders in the KIPP network are empowered to design their schools as they wish, so blended learning would never be imposed top-down across the charter-school chain. Richard Barth notes that "the way things spread in KIPP is viral. The key to expanding an idea is that people try something and then it works. I can't put it any more simply than that."

Because blended learning seems to be working, KIPP Empower Academy's results have sparked interest from other school leaders who are starting fresh KIPP schools or revamping old ones. KIPP Chicago had already ventured into blended learning during the 2010–2011 school year with two pilot programs, funded in part by Gates Foundation grants aimed at encouraging numerous blended-learning pilots in existing charter-school chains. The Chicago pilots took place in eighth grade at KIPP Ascend Middle School, and in first grade at KIPP Ascend Primary School. These schools found that a "power hour" modeled on Rocketship's original Learning Lab setup was the most successful for them. So students go to a computer lab for instruction, and then are pulled out into small groups.

Based on good results at these two pilots, all KIPP Chicago students are being exposed to blended learning in some form during the 2012–2013 school year. A fully blended-learning school called KIPP Create College Prep Middle School opened in fall 2012 to serve 90 fifth graders. It will use both the power-hour model and a rotational model in classrooms throughout the day, and grow to 350 students by fall 2015.

KIPP NYC also opened a blended-learning school, KIPP Washington Heights Middle School, in fall 2012, with a focus on math. Students attend 60-minute math classes, starting with a short "Do Now" exercise, and then split into groups. One group works with the teacher while the others work on math exercises on the computers. The idea is to have multiple mini-lessons per class, tailored to students who need reinforcement on certain concepts.

Other Schools

While the best-known examples of blended-learning schools have been nurtured with philanthropic help, blended learning is a broad and grass-roots movement that is surging into schools even when there is no support from donors or education-reform groups. Thurgood Marshall Middle School is located in Los Angeles, about three miles north of KIPP Empower Academy, and is housed in a space that also functions as a Pentecostal church. Principal Peter Watts heard about blended learning, and realized that he'd done a form of blended learning himself: his master's degree is from the University of Phoenix, the for-profit institution of higher learning that enrolls hundreds of thousands of students each year, mixing computer instruction with some face-to-face components (in what might qualify as an "enriched virtual" model).

Intending to bring blended learning to his school, Watts asked Apple what it would cost to get new laptops for all his students. The price—$300,000—was far outside his budget. Watts had no deep-pocket backers, but he persevered, in the process becoming a leader in showing that blended learning can be implemented on a shoestring budget.

"My teachers and I all sat down and asked: how can we do this blended learning within our school budget?" They found dozens of old computers in the church's basement. "We inventoried every computer on campus. We were taking keyboards and mice off teachers' desks." Watts had the computers refurbished as best he could. He decided to focus solely on math, using Khan Academy because it was free, and Revolution Prep because he was able to purchase it through money allocated for after-school programs and tutoring.

Needless to say, this completely bootstrapped approach to blended learning isn't perfect. Some of the computers turned out to be lemons, and the shortage of well-functioning machines has been frustrating for Watts and his students. As a supplement, Watts managed to find money for a program to help families purchase computers for their homes, which students use for homework.

But the fascinating part of all this is that even in the absence of reliable computers, blended learning is helping the Thurgood Marshall teachers do their jobs better. They get reasonably useful data on their kids. A handful of seventh-grade students have already moved ahead to algebra after showing they've mastered pre-algebra. "In a traditional setting, they would have just stayed where they were with the rest of the class," says Watts.

Other students are getting more practice on what the school now knows for sure they didn't learn the first time. In the past, Thurgood Marshall would have put all eighth graders into algebra. After looking at data from their blended-learning program though, Watts said they realized it "would be crazy for us to put them in algebra. They're not ready." Instead, these eighth graders started with algebra readiness, with kids moving ahead or not moving ahead as the data indicated.

So what do the students think? "The kids do like it overall," says Watts. "There are some kids who say 'I want my textbook back! I don't want to use the computer that much!'" But for the most part, "they feel like the teacher has access to them more than in the past." They also like "knowing exactly where they are and not having to wait for a teacher to give them a grade." Kids see what they need to work on, and "teachers have been embracing the data." This is "the first year where they've not had to explain why a child got the grade they received. Parents know why their child is getting this grade, because they've seen the data themselves."

Thurgood Marshall Middle School has one thing in common with other schools that enjoy more robustly funded blended programs: it is a charter school. Charter schools tend to have operational flexibility that can be crucial to establishing a blended experiment. Yet while charter schools are growing rapidly in number, and while vehicles such as the Charter School Growth Fund exist to help them expand, after 20 years their market share is still in the single digits. The lion's share of American students continue to attend traditional public schools operated directly by large school districts. So many philanthropists wonder if it is possible to launch blended-learning programs in traditional district schools.

California's Rogers Family Foundation is attempting to find out. Carrie Douglass, who directed much of the foundation's attempt to bring blended learning into a conventional public school district, says that "it seemed that most of the blended-learning investment and innovation was going into charter schools. That makes sense in many ways"—after all, many foundations worry with good reason that a large gift given through the front door of a district will simply disappear into general operations—"but we feel like we will miss the boat with the power of this reform if we don't get into districts early with really thoughtful and comprehensive pilots."

Because there is evidence it works, blended learning is a grassroots movement surging into schools, even when there is no support from the establishment.

After years of generous, focused philanthropy, the Rogers Foundation has much political capital in the Oakland Unified School District, which has long struggled with a high dropout rate and disappointing test results. So when the foundation "reached out to schools we've funded in the past," says Douglass, and said "we're interested in making this investment. If you're interested, let us know," several district schools responded. In the fall of 2012, four district schools—Elmhurst Community Prep, EnCompass Academy, Korematsu Discovery Academy and Madison Middle School—launched blended-learning pilots.

Rogers and its partners (who are working directly with the schools, and are maintaining financial control of the operation) are investing $1 million to support design, implementation, and follow-up. The Stanford Research Institute is studying the Oakland pilots for results. "Something as important to us as student achievement is that teachers are happier and more effective," says Douglass. "Teacher turnover is a huge problem in Oakland. Our goal for the first year is that these pilot teachers would go out and tell other teachers

Many philanthropists wonder if it is possible to launch blended-learning programs in traditional district schools.

that they need to try this." Testimony like that could make blended learning adoption a viral phenomenon.

Despite having to work within the constraints of the existing school model in terms of class sizes, bell schedules, and room size—all things they'd like to have the opportunity to rework—the foundation's pilot has so far been able to deliver on its basic promises. They hope next to increase the academic rigor of the program, and there is a huge need for training so teachers can better evaluate data on their students, and help kids use programs.

The foundation will be extending the program to a second cohort of schools next year. The new group will include some charter schools as well as conventional district-run schools. The Rogers Foundation knows that this experiment is risky, but given how many students continue to receive their education in districts like Oakland, they think it's also an experiment that needs to be run.

Rhode Island, with philanthropic help, is likewise experimenting with blended learning in district schools. Deborah Gist, Rhode Island's Education Commissioner, uses multiple devices herself to accomplish her work and maintains a presence in social media. Expanding the use of technology in Rhode Island schools was thus on her agenda.

With support from the Hume and Peters foundations, Gist's department decided to host a blended-learning conference in February 2012. Roughly 300 educators and other stakeholders from almost every district in the state gathered to hear from national experts on the topic. After the conference, about a dozen schools applied for a mostly taxpayer-funded grant to implement a blended-learning program.

The education department chose Pleasantview Elementary in Providence, which is one of the state's "persistently lowest-achieving schools in one of the highest poverty neighborhoods," according to state officials. (The state is also pursuing other grant money to make blended programs a reality at some of the other schools who applied.) The Pleasantview staff went through extensive professional development over the summer, and the school acquired enough equipment to have about a 1-to-1 ratio of students to computers. The grant will be implemented over two years. The school program will be studied closely, and if it produces good results, will be copied elsewhere.

Under the leadership of former schools chancellor Joel Klein, New York City also implemented a blended-learning model in several district schools through a program called the School of One. For now, the program covers just math, and it started as a summer-only pilot before being extended to other schools. Students learn in a large, open space with several stations. Some kids work with teachers; some work online, and some in groups. Each day, the kids take quizzes to determine what they should learn the next day.

An intriguingly data-driven experiment, School of One used an algorithm to create a personalized plan for math instruction for each student, drawing from thousands of lessons pulled from over 50 providers. The chosen software could change daily based on assessment. The Broad Foundation was an early supporter of the program and its creator Joel Rose. "We found it interesting largely because of its use of data to alter the kind of instruction a student gets based on what they need," says Luis de la Fuente, a director at the Broad Foundation. "It's not like it was changing the whole set-up of how a student goes to school, but it was beginning to innovate for one subject and pushing the envelope of what school could look like."

Initial results were mixed. The algorithm didn't completely account for the human factor in education. "We've gotten some criticism from teachers and parents on how that worked—that it was too in the weeds—and that they had not done a good job of creating more critical thinking opportunities for students," says de la Fuente. Students also seemed to crave "lasting relationship time" with one teacher, even if pure data analysis suggested that was not the optimal way to be spending any unit of time.

Of the three schools that tried it, one did better than peer schools, one did the same and one did worse. Since the program is limited to math, it's clear that other issues in the schools experimenting with it colored the overall results. Ultimately, two of the schools that tried it dropped the program, though others adopted it.

Lessons learned during the first experiment were used to improve classroom practices. And in the second year, results were clearly positive. The most recent outcomes show School of One students posting twice the gains in proficiency level of kids at middle schools citywide. While the project's ultimate outcomes are not yet clear, it is being watched closely by donors and others anxious to bring innovation to traditional urban school districts.

Founder Joel Rose makes it clear that his team is still making discoveries and improving rapidly through trial and error. "We've been at this three years, and while we're learning things every day about things like the

> "We've had the old model of schooling for 170 years—finding a new solution won't happen in one fell swoop," says Joel Rose.

logarithm and schedule, we're still only 50 percent baked." For instance, the process of evaluating the day's work by students and creating their work schedule for the following day initially took 10 hours, but over the course of three years the process has been automated and now requires roughly five minutes. "We've had the old model of schooling for 170 years—finding a new solution won't happen in one fell swoop," he notes.

Rose's spinoff organization, New Classrooms, is continually modifying the program, and has expanded its "Teach to One" model more broadly into eight schools in three different cities during the 2012–2013 school year. The CityBridge Foundation, for instance, helped bring the program to Washington, D.C., in fall 2012.

As the School of One experiment shows, innovation is sometimes messy. Some new ideas don't work in quite the way you think they will. Openness to experimentation is needed. One of the big reasons education reformers have generally worked with charter schools is that trying something new in an existing bureaucracy is hard. Existing organizations, especially large ones, are seldom able to adopt changes that upend their whole business model, notes Clayton Christensen in his analysis of disruptive innovations. Settled life is just too comfortable to take new chances.

Charter schools are often new schools, and districts don't open many new schools. But sometimes they do. In particular, districts can, these days, tap federal funds to close failing schools and re-open them as turnaround schools.

Sajan George worked in district turnaround efforts during his years at business-advisory firm Alvarez & Marsal, and after leaving, he founded Matchbook Learning, a nonprofit that implements blended learning at turnaround schools. With funding from the NewSchools Venture Fund and others, Matchbook Learning is attempting to turn around two Detroit public schools. The A. L. Holmes school started a blended-learning model during the 2011–2012 school year, and Brenda Scott Academy reopened with blended learning in the fall of 2012.

These Detroit schools face big challenges. Turnaround schools tend to be in the bottom 5 percent of performance, and many students are incredibly far behind, testing at the first- or second-grade level in seventh grade, George reports. But "they're going from zero to something," he says. At A. L. Holmes, eight out of ten students gained at least 10 percent on annual standardized tests. Of those, three out of ten made gains of more than 30 percent.

As of this book's writing, Brenda Scott Academy was only a few months into its experiment, but families are voting with their feet. With bad publicity as a turnaround school, enrollment dropped from 832 in spring 2012 to 650 in fall 2012. But by December, enrollment was back up to 932, George reports. "We have kids showing up every day enrolling," he says. Families "really see the value" because "you don't have to be middle-income or highly educated to understand that your kids need to embrace technology in learning if they're going to be competitive for jobs."

The desire to help children compete in a high-tech world played a part in the decision of Mooresville, North Carolina, to adopt blended learning district wide. The district repurposed existing textbook and technology funding (with no net increase in costs) to adopt a 1-to-1 ratio of laptops to students. Students do much of their work online, with programs set at the level that students need. Constant data from the programs keep teachers and parents better informed, and help keep students from falling through the cracks. Tech facilitators at each school mentor teachers and work with them to figure out how to teach in this new way. It seems to be working. While the district has one of the lowest per-pupil funding budgets in the state, its test scores have risen over the past few years from middle of the pack to near the top—evidence that innovative districts, like charter schools, can do more with less. There may be a role for local donors in encouraging traditional school districts in their area to study the Mooresville experience.

The Potential of
Blended Learning

Most of the blended-learning programs described in the last chapter use some form of rotation model—what Heather Staker, co-author of the Innosight taxonomy, calls "a sustaining innovation" rather than a disruptive one. At least some of the normal classroom structure remains the same. So what about all the other models described by Innosight in the first pages of chapter 1? Do they exist anywhere in robust forms?

Some do. Two of Staker's children attend Acton Academy in Austin, Texas, a private school that she'd classify as a "flex" model. Students use popular software such as DreamBox for math, Rosetta Stone for language, SpellingCity for spelling, and so forth. Students establish their own learning goals for this flex time with help from their teachers. "The thing I like about blended learning, and that made me want it for my kids, is that it's so much more efficient if implemented correctly," Staker says. "It frees up a lot of extra space for the great things schools can be doing"—like small-group discussions and project-based learning. Indeed, Staker moved from Honolulu to Austin mostly to enroll her children in Acton, a school she learned about while writing the Innosight white paper *The Rise of K–12 Blended Learning*. "It was really hard to be reading about all of these programs—I thought I had arrived upon a truth—and still be sending my own children to a traditional school," she says.

Most states now have virtual schools. The Florida Virtual School, the North Carolina Virtual Public School (NCVPS) and others enable the last two of the blended-learning models: the self-blend and the enhanced virtual models. In North Carolina, for instance, a student who does not have access to Mandarin Chinese or Arabic in her home school can enroll in these courses through NCVPS. Some students enroll in these schools full-time; the NCVPS website contains a testimonial from a mother whose child had broken her leg and was unable to attend school for several months. By keeping up with courses online, she graduated on time and with honors. These schools will have a growing role in any education mix, and could potentially be completely transformative, perhaps spawning an even bigger home-schooling revolution, or "one-room internet school-houses" where communities create co-ops to supervise small groups of children while the parents work and the kids all learn online.

Many foundations say they'd love to see and fund additional blended-learning schools, and particularly new and more innovative forms of schools. At present they tend to see proposals for more of the same: often three-station classroom rotational models. As grantees would point out, though, this is a circular problem; when educational entrepreneurs see existing models getting funded, they propose more of the same. "You can't keep asking me for a track record," says Ben Rayer, a veteran school leader who launched Merit Prep, a blended-learning charter school, in Newark in fall 2012, as part of an organization he intends to expand nationally. "If you want to see innovation and experimentation, you can't get that from people who are doing what they're doing today."

Tom Vander Ark, author of *Getting Smart: How Digital Learning is Changing the World*, says that this educational frontier "would really benefit from more successful models. For somebody who writes about this and talks about this, I sound like a broken record on Carpe Diem and Rocketship." Vander Ark notes, "I love those guys," but believes there are many additional possible variations between their respective examples.

Educators working in blended schools themselves also think it's important to push the field's boundaries in new directions. Diego Arambula, the principal at Summit Rainier, says, "We've seen some hesitancy in people on the ground to truly do something wild and creative and different that could potentially be better for kids."

Part of the problem is that ethical educators are always properly worried about experimenting with children. Even if they learn a great deal from an experiment, trying something truly radical risks leaving kids worse off. While a school in crisis might be willing to try anything, what if a school is muddling along in a reasonable fashion? You can't blame parents for being wary of a 48-to-1, or 75-to-1, pupil-to-teacher ratio, numbers that sound, to conventional ears not attuned to the new possibilities of digital learning, like they'd invite chaos.

But timidity and stagnation isn't inevitable. One approach is to ditch the idea of multi-year, rigid experiments. Diane Tavenner, the Summit schools head, suggests "there is a space where you can balance responsibly experimenting and moving things forward, allowing small failures so you really learn."

In the software world, beta-testing involves releasing advanced but probably flawed programs to small numbers of early adopters to see what works and what doesn't. This is a good mindset for education reformers, too. Blended-learning programs can be beta-tested, and if a certain class configuration or software package isn't working—which you'll be able to see fairly quickly from the results data—you can change it.

This is already happening today. At Merit Prep in Newark, Rayer started the school year in fall 2012 with a schedule that concentrated most of the teacher collaboration and planning time on Fridays. But he soon realized that this left teachers quite frazzled the rest of the week, with little time to grab a snack or even go to the bathroom. So "we had to change our entire schedule right after Thanksgiving," he says. An early agreement to work with a partner who would build better data tools didn't pan out. So teachers are now working on creating their own tools for visualizing how each student is doing. The goal is to come up with one or two metrics each week that can be gleaned from the software and are relevant to student performance. Two to three will survive each month, with the goal of going into the next school year with

10–15 measures that staff can then work to improve upon. "Hopefully we're not going backwards," says Rayer, but "we're trying to flip school on its head," and consequently, "there's a lot of experimenting going on."

Educational technology software that can advance blended learning is also being beta-tested. Heather Gilchrist runs Socratic Labs, an ed-tech accelerator in New York City. Her company has close ties with the New York City schools, and with Columbia's Teachers College, and so "before we build stuff . . . we're first validating that there's an actual problem." Teachers partner with her to be matched up with a tech entrepreneur. They work together to "test a solution with a small group. Then we can scale it."

Sometimes all this trial and error is frustrating. Diane Tavenner notes that she gets tour groups coming through Summit schools two or three times per week. "They're expecting to walk into something magical," she says, "something that's kind of mind-blowing." But "there are days when it looks terrible because you're trying something that doesn't work."

Small failures are part of the scientific process. Indeed, many entrepreneurs embrace the idea of failing fast and often. Matt Candler's 4.0 Schools design lab opened in New Orleans in 2010, and encourages education entrepreneurs to start small and develop solid ideas before even getting to the stage of starting a capital-intensive school or launching a company to sell things to the broader world. He draws parallels to entrepreneurs in the food industry. Rather than having the mindset of opening a restaurant, "food trucks are an interesting concept to apply to education," he says. A food truck is low-cost and flexible. Likewise, education ideas can be tested in after-school programs, in summer programs, or in pop-up schools serving working parents faced with the problem of what to do with your kids during spring break if you can't get those days off. "You can learn a lot about blended learning without me asking you for $5 million to launch my blended-learning charter operation," Candler says.

The other mindset change is to keep repeating "Web 1.0." As the internet became a major reality in modern life by the late 1990s, people were still unsure how best to use it. Companies created webpages that simply regurgitated the same content from their brochures. There was little of the interactivity and the constant updates that we now know works best online.

Likewise, Blended Learning 1.0 schools are just hinting at what can happen when technology is diligently applied to improve instruction and learning. Ever more innovative models just now being dreamed up may place the fulcrum of technology in a different place and improve performance dramatically. A decade from now, many of these innovations are likely to seem obvious, but they aren't at present. "We assume learning takes place in a classroom, with one teacher, from 7 a.m. to 3 p.m. each day," says Caprice Young, vice president for education at the Laura and John Arnold Foundation. "With blended learning, we need to actively identify preconceived notions that constrain—and knock them down."

One role philanthropy can play is to support educational entrepreneurs as they tinker with fresh techniques, structures, and content. The Next Generation Learning Challenges competition funded by the Bill & Melinda Gates Foundation and the William and Flora Hewlett Foundation will fund (with grants up to $1 million) 20 new schools with blended models, all committed to students spending at least 25 percent of their time online while pursuing aggressive goals like a year and a half of math or reading progress in a single school year, while being studied by experts keen on repeating what works. "I was pleasantly surprised by the diversity and level of innovation of the applicants," says Gates' Scott Benson.

Even before more innovative experiments are launched in the real world, we can examine the potential power of blended learning and understand why it excites creative educators, and encourages them to think it may have power to transform thousands of schools for the better. There are four major theoretical benefits that experts see in blended learning: individualization, improved feedback, teacher effectiveness and satisfaction, and cost control. New-style schools that harness even one of these could reap crisp payoffs. Models that successfully deploy several or all of these advantages could create dramatic improvement over traditional schools.

Lever 1: Individualization
The technology at the heart of blended-learning programs offers unprecedented opportunities for personalized instruction, at one's own pace and style, in the way that an individual tutor might direct a child. This has all sorts of implications for students—particularly those on the far ends of the performance spectrum. With good computerized lessons, students who are struggling to master concepts can be offered almost unlimited opportunities to repeat and reinterpret new material, all without standing out or feeling embarrassed about sidetracking the rest of the class.

Likewise, students who have command of a particular subject are able to move onto something fresh without delay or unnecessary repetition. One problem with the No Child Left Behind ethic, which grades schools by how well they do at pulling up their weakest students, is that schools and teachers ignore kids capable of zooming ahead. High-potential students

"All my students are learning at different rates. . . . A huge misconception is that everybody needs to be at exactly the same spot," notes teacher Wendy Chaves.

have performed much less well than other students over the last decade or so, and are particularly underserved in schools where many students struggle to meet grade-level standards. With schools judged mostly on whether kids meet minimum standards, what incentive is there to spend time on a child capable of exceeding the minimum without any assistance? Teachers often feel guilty about wasted potential and bored students. Indeed, that word "guilt" comes up frequently in conversations with educators. But teachers only have so much time.

Blended learning promises to start solving this problem without grouping the top-performing students in their own schools or classes—a practice that advocates see as best, but that schools often resist for philosophical and logistical reasons. As educators at Summit discovered, making mixed-ability classes work in practice isn't a walk in the park, but it is theoretically possible. Adaptive software of the sort that Knewton, DreamBox, and other ed-tech start-ups are rolling out should be able to meet a child right where he is.

Just because you're physically sitting in a fifth-grade math class doesn't mean you need to be doing fifth-grade math. If you need to work on second-grade skills, that's fine, and if you can zoom ahead to trigonometry, that's great too. As you move forward showing mastery, teachers can keep challenging you. Within a regular classroom, differentiating like this is extremely hard, even for the best of teachers.

Adaptive software can do that sort of differentiating automatically. Much as Netflix or Amazon or Pandora are able to learn from each user's actions to predict what that person will next need or desire, so adaptive educational software can pick up how a given student learns, and what he or she is missing. That allows the instruction to become more effective as time passes. The lessons presented to students begin to differ, and teachers get suggestions on which resources they might try to get through problems with that pupil, based on his particular learning history. There will be multiple paths for students to learn and demonstrate mastery of the same concept.

Wendy Chaves, who teaches at ATAMS in Los Angeles, says she was "like two different people"—the Wendy who taught using traditional tools, and the

Wendy who intelligently exploited technology. "I was a pretty good teacher," she says. "Then I came here and realized how much I was doing a disservice to my students. I thought I was good and I realized I wasn't. I was only reaching 35 percent of my class. That's not the way I should have been teaching."

It was a "really harsh realization," she says. "There definitely needs to be a lot of training with blended learning. I was not prepared for the model whatsoever." Yet when she started teaching with the benefit of data, she found that her classes were collectively doing much better, "even though all my students are learning at different rates. They're not all going to be at the same spot. That's a huge misconception—that everybody needs to be exactly at the same spot."

Blended-learning teachers must make their peace with this heterogeneity—which has always existed, but often been hidden in mass-taught classes. Under blended learning, students only move on when they've demonstrated mastery. "They're learning at their own speed," notes Chaves. "You kind of have to relinquish control."

This individualization is the breakthrough that, at Khan Academy, "we're most interested in—really personalizing the education for the student," says Shantanu Sinha, the academy's president and chief operating officer. Much of the original media attention on Sal Khan focused on his videos and the concept of "flipping" the classroom: the idea that students would watch video lectures at home, and then do traditional "homework"—problem sets and assignments—in class. In Sinha's vision of education, teachers become "great mentors for each student individually. A lot of people misunderstand. It's not so much about watching videos at home and doing exercises in the classroom. That could be one component of what happens. But it's more about personalizing education and making classrooms as interactive as possible." Customizing lessons to each learner, he says, as the increasingly adaptive Khan problem sets make possible, is "the core of why we're working with schools. It's the whole thing. We didn't go in just to use our videos instead of teachers lecturing. There's nothing truly innovative about that."

Teachers will need to rethink their approach in order to capture the potential of blended learning. Sinha notes that some teachers first use Khan Academy mate-

All children deserve to be challenged—to work at a pace that introduces them to the joys of working hard to understand something.

Technology is a great equalizer. The best programs will soon be available to urban, suburban, and rural schools alike.

rials to "augment exactly what a student was going to do anyway." Students still go through the same concept matter in the same calendar week, just as the teacher has always proceeded. "The teacher is still setting the pace for the student." When that happens, we're "seeing improvements, and it's still helpful—it's better than the model of worksheets. But it's not as great as it can be."

The real magic happens when teachers decide that "I will let my students run with it," says Sinha. "I'm not going to hold you back." Then, students enter the driver's seat on the pace and form of what they're learning. Not only is the instruction better tailored to their personal strengths and weaknesses, but because they have more control, student motivation and engagement tends to rise.

That philosophy is slowly spreading to many schools that use Khan Academy to supplement their traditional instruction. As Jesse Roe at Summit says, "our hope is to individualize to the point where we really don't know what grade the student is in." With Khan math sequences running uninterruptedly from the concept of 1+1 all the way to calculus, there are no obvious stopping points associated with grades. And so, teachers tell of kids doing advanced work at remarkably early ages. Teacher Rekha Pardeshi, on the Khan Academy website, describes her fourth-grade class at Stratford School in California where "all students have completed the arithmetic challenge, 10 have completed the pre-algebra challenge, six have completed the trigonometry challenge, three have completed the algebra challenge" and one even earned the calculus badge.

Very few schools could offer a fourth grader the time and opportunity to experiment with calculus, or would even imagine that she'd be capable of comprehending it. But if the child wants to learn, why shouldn't she? Technology can provide quality control in a way you don't really get by sticking an advanced child in the back of the room with a special textbook.

All children deserve to be challenged. All children deserve to work at a pace that introduces them to the joys of working hard to understand something. Perhaps the biggest way schools fail bright children is by letting them think education should be easy. When they finally do encounter challenging work, perhaps at college or in the workforce, they become risk averse and don't know what to make of it. They don't know how to toil harder and try different approaches until they finally master something that seemed outside their reach.

Just as emphatically, many education reformers are excited about blended learning for its potential to raise the test scores of kids who have fallen behind their peers, and are really struggling with average-level material. As Sal Khan says, "I think this problem—the one-pace-fits-all lecture or curriculum—is even more damaging for remedial classes. People's gaps are all over the place. With an advanced class, you're more confident the foundation material is in place."[1] Remedial students need to have the holes in their knowledge carefully probed and then backfilled, something computerized instruction excels at, particular when matched with in-person tutoring informed by up-to-the-minute data reports.

And so, paradoxically, blended learning offers opportunities to eliminate one of the oldest tensions in teaching: Should the instructor teach to the lowest common denominator, address the average level, or reach for peak performance? With blended learning there is the potential to serve all students well at the same time.

Finally, technology is a great equalizer. As the educational software market develops, the best programs will be available to urban, suburban, and rural schools alike. Expense is no barrier to having a good blended-learning program; the best ones can actually be substantially cheaper than traditional teaching. And so blended learning can make personalization of the sort that well-to-do families have always been able to access through tutoring available to children from all backgrounds. That's one reason donors who are passionate about a broad distribution of education resources are particularly excited about what technology can do here.

Lever 2: Improved Feedback

Schools are supposed to help children get better at certain skills or areas of knowledge. But how, exactly, do people improve at things?

The old saying is that practice makes perfect, but this can't be just any kind of practice. Schools that mass-assign worksheets every night often fail to see measurable results from such labors other than unhappy kids and parents. Simple repetition isn't enough. Author Geoff Colvin notes that "extensive research in a wide range of fields shows that many people not only fail to become outstandingly good at what they do, no matter how many years they spend doing it, they frequently don't even get any better than they were when they started."[2]

---

1. Laura Vanderkam, "The Math of Khan," *City Journal*, Winter 2012.
2. Geoff Colvin, *Talent is Overrated* (New York: Penguin, 2008).

Real improvement requires something called "deliberate practice." This form of intense training has long been used by virtuoso musicians and athletes to improve, but is remarkably absent from how most of us tackle new skills and ideas at school. It involves figuring out exactly what you know, and what you don't.

Perhaps your left-handed arpeggios are weak, or you choke up on short putts. You practice these skills over and over again with someone or something right there giving you constant and, ideally, *instant* feedback. Professional athletes, for instance, have coaches on top of them if any attempt was better or worse than the last one. They spend many hours watching recordings of their performances so they can learn from each attempt. Skiers work in wind-tunnels to hone their form and get instant feedback on what boosts speed. A stand-up comedian gets feedback trying out his material in small clubs before doing a major show. "Deliberate practice is hard," Colvin writes. "It hurts. But it works. More of it equals better performance. Tons of it equals great performance."

Needless to say, this kind of deliberate practice is rare in most schools, at least on the academic side. Students do problem sets, but they only see days later if the approach they used was right or wrong. And if it was wrong, they have to wait for time with the teacher to grasp why.

Feedback requires a lot of work from teachers. Picture a middle-school instructor assigning a grammar worksheet to the 96 students who come through her four English classes each day. If she puts a mere two minutes into each worksheet, that's more than three hours (192 minutes) of work for her. Unless the school has put money in the budget for grading help, she simply can't assign more than a few such assessments per week. And the students probably won't all get feedback from her the next day, let alone instantaneously, on where their grammar is right or wrong. Alex Hernandez of the Charter School Growth Fund points out that "a teacher could stay up 24 hours a day grading papers and not give the feedback that kids get in 10 minutes playing a video game." In a conventional classroom, the feedback loop is sluggish, if not broken.

Intensive time in a computer lab, though, has much in common with those video games. In many blended schools, students are getting up to two hours per day of what looks pretty similar to deliberate practice: work that is right at the student's level, software that points out exactly what the child is getting wrong, and then the opportunity to practice those skills again until she understands and shows mastery. When musicians get two hours per day of deliberate practice, they start improving dramatically. Is it any wonder that children who get two hours per day of deliberate practice at computer stations also improve?

> A teacher could stay up 24 hours a day grading papers and not give the feedback on what each child has mastered and where he's failing that 10 minutes playing a video game provides.

Any academic outcome that involves skills can benefit from practice of this sort. Math is an obvious application, but writing involves grammar skills—and these can be practiced too; a new software program called NoRedInk, launched from the Imagine K–12 business incubator, takes this instant-feedback concept to the matter of subject-verb agreement. Foreign languages benefit from practice in speaking and writing. Basic science skills, which often involve math, or lab procedures, can be practiced in the same way that basketball players can do sprinting and jumping drills.

To be sure, not all of this involves higher-order thinking. But the promise of blended learning is that by having computers take over basic skills practice, doing it quickly and efficiently so students can reap the benefits of a higher volume of practice, teacher time can be preserved for nurturing critical thinking. A teacher who doesn't have to assign and grade grammar worksheets can spend her time prodding students to think about what makes an appealing essay topic, and why certain opening sentences are more effective than others. She will operate more like a tutor or leadership coach, less like a drill sergeant. This is a very big shift in educational practice, and one with profound possibilities for improving both the quality and the rewards of teaching.

Lever 3: Teacher Effectiveness and Satisfaction

This changing allocation of teacher time gets at the third major benefit of blended learning: a far more satisfying teaching experience, at least for teachers who embrace the idea of using technology to be more productive. The definition of a tool is something that makes it easier to accomplish a given task. In a blended-learning regime, technology makes teaching easier and more efficient. If someone went into the teaching profession to make a difference in children's lives, which presumably most teachers did, having effective tools can make all the difference in the world.

Think of it this way: 150 years ago, the best doctor in the world could be compassionate and hard working, and spend hours honing his skills, and he would still be radically less effective than an average doctor today. Access to basic diagnostic tools and medicines we now take for granted have dramatically improved outcomes. If our 1860s doctor had expected to regularly help people live long and healthy lives, he would become jaded and burnt out over time, as even his best efforts could produce only marginal improvements.

Much literature exists on the importance of teacher quality. Parents instinctively know that it matters; KIPP co-founder Dave Levin polled audience members at a Philanthropy Roundtable event on blended learning about whether they'd prefer a smaller class with a mediocre teacher or a larger one with an excellent teacher, and the results were overwhelming for the latter. But when judging teachers we should remember the analogy between the best Civil War doctors and today's average doctors. Updated tools can make a teacher better in a way he or she might not at first even be able to comprehend. When teachers first discover all the data they can get from blended learning, says Peter Watts, the principal of Thurgood Marshall School, they "are afraid of it." Teachers discover that their pupils have all sorts of gaps in their knowledge. "They believe it says something about who you are as a teacher."

Watts says he has had teachers fretting with him that "the data say I'm doing horribly." He found himself assuring his staff: "You may need some professional development, but you're not a horrible teacher. We'll provide the training and support you need to be the best teacher possible." Then it's the teacher's responsibility to figure out what instructional strategies work best to help each child fill in the holes in his or her understanding.

Teachers who adapt to this growth mindset and see the possibilities of blended learning often love the result. They're busy people, and appreciate anything that takes mounds of low-value work off their plates. Juan Nuñez, one of Watts' teachers at Thurgood Marshall, recalls that "when I got my first exposure to these types of resources, a light went on. 'I don't need to grade stuff?'"

The technology also allows teachers to see concrete evidence of progress. Wendy Chaves, the math teacher at ATAMS, notes that watching her students getting better at the skills she's teaching has "been amazing. Being able to track the data has been a great thing, not only for us, but the students can see, and their parents can see, their progress. They're always improving, every single day."

The new visibility of information may be starker for parents than any other participant in the education process. They can get regular emails showing exact details of their child's performance. No more guessing as to whether Johnny is keeping up.

And Chaves notes that "the beauty about it is, we know it's going to get better" as the technology improves and teachers become more skilled at using it. To be sure, this involves growing pains. One has to teach in some new ways.

On the first day of a pilot blended-learning math program in a fourth-grade classroom at Visitation Catholic school in North Philadelphia, teacher Mary Anne Corcoran is working hard to figure this out. With 16 kids in the class, half are supposed to be working on DreamBox, and half with her. But with only five machines up and running, she has the class in three groups: computer, teacher, and individual work.

The DreamBox kids have headsets; the group doing problem sets in their workbooks does not. Corcoran starts out in usual teacher mode, up at the chalkboard using her teacher voice to instruct her small group. Naturally, the individual-work group finds their teacher far more interesting than their pencils and workbooks, and they start watching her instead. Seeing this, she swiftly abandons the chalkboard, and moves closer to her instructional group, speaking much more softly.

You also have to "change students' mindset about what learning looks like," says Summit math teacher Jesse Roe. Students must be taught to take control of their own learning. That is by no means automatic. Skeptics have

> Students must be taught to take control of their own learning.

sometimes walked into new blended-learning classrooms and noted students clicking listlessly through multiple-choice questions. If the skeptic is a reporter wishing to write a negative story on charter schools or new educational technology, such scenes provide plenty of fodder.

But when teachers flip the motivation switch, the transformation is pretty exhilarating, says Roe. "You're shifting the flow of information and content away from teachers giving, to students finding. They're looking it up online, asking friends, asking the teacher."

Thanks to the oceans of data a good blended-learning program produces, "we know right away if they're understanding something," says Roe. If the child isn't catching on, the teacher has a conversation with her about other strategies for finding the answer, and about persisting until success is achieved. As Roe puts it, the teacher says, "I know this was really difficult for you, but look at what progress we've made. The frustration turns more into a natural feeling—this is what it feels like to learn something new." At Summit, "we felt that kind of mindset was how the best critical thinkers and learners think as adults. We wanted to foster that in our kids." This struggle toward mastery gives teachers the chance to experience what many went into teaching for: producing "aha!" moments in children, moments that often occur during the tightly focused individual interactions that blended learning allows teachers to have with students.

In normal classes, there is little time for individual interaction, as the teacher tries to keep everyone focused on the same material. Keeping a group of children's attention requires heroic efforts, or at least a magician's bag of tricks. Doug Lemov's book *Teach Like a Champion* provides a fascinating taxonomy of the traditional tools experienced teachers pick up for keeping children on task. You cold call on students. You do call and response lessons. You move around the classroom to show you command it, breaking the invisible barrier between the first row of desks and the space in front of the board. But why should running a classroom be limited by the demands of crowd control? Teaching is about pedagogy, not herding cattle.

Meanwhile, parents know that it's nearly impossible to break a kid away from a screen that has something interesting on it. As John Danner from Rocketship puts it, "If programs are engaging, kids actually seem to have very long attention spans." Indeed, kids sometimes have long attention spans even when programs aren't so interesting. Kids love looking at computers. Even classes with 48 children—16 on computers, 16 doing projects together, 16 getting teacher instruction—can be quieter and better managed than attempting to direct the attention of 24 children to the same thing at the same time.

Does that mean that blended learning relies on electronic babysitting? Sure, but if you don't think schools are already doing this with films and TV and uncoordinated computer use, think again. And in this case, the babysitter is also practicing phonics and multiplication with the kids, instructing while keeping them quiet so the teacher can do her highest-value work of getting quality time with each student in turn. The electronic babysitter augments what the teacher can do—and hence makes the teacher more effective. As Danner told the *Christian Science Monitor*: "Kindergarten teachers didn't sign up to be kindergarten teachers because they wanted to teach short 'a' and long 'a' sounds for 80 hours. They signed up because they like working with children. They like to teach social emotional skills, to stretch their thinking."[3]

---

3. Jina Moore, "Change Agent: John Danner Shoots for the Stars with Rocketship Charter Schools," *Christian Science Monitor*, September 1, 2011, http://www.csmonitor.com/World/Making-a-difference/Change-Agent/2011/0901/ John-Danner-shoots-for-the-stars-with-Rocketship-charter-schools.

It is true that, over time, widespread adoption of blended learning may require fewer teachers, with these teachers being assisted by instructional aides. In a hospital, much of the basic work of checking temperatures and blood pressure is done by nursing assistants. People understand that it makes little sense to send a surgeon around every few hours to do this. Yet teachers with masters degrees are grading spelling tests. Education should experience the same specialization that other sectors of the economy have, with skills properly matched to the task to make the most efficient use of scarce resources.

Ideally, blended learning will allow a smaller number of truly wonderful teachers to preside over more students. Bryan Hassel of Public Impact calls these teachers "3X" teachers for their ability to have three times the impact of low-performing teachers. This isn't an exaggeration; studies have found that

Increased teacher satisfaction may be the catalyst that truly spreads blended learning in schools.

repeated exposure to excellent teachers can help students from lower socio-economic backgrounds close the achievement gap. The problem is that if you insist on having only 20 or 25 students in a class, there just aren't enough 3X teachers to go around. Ideally, with blended learning, the field won't have to rely on so many mediocre teachers, because less-complicated (if sometimes onerous) work will be outsourced to assistants. These teacher-aide positions, freed of the heavy credentialing demands of traditional teaching, will appeal to a different group, drawn in by aspects like the part-time work week, which may appeal to parents of young children.

While a somewhat smaller teacher corps might be problematic for those collecting union dues from teachers, it's less clear that it would be a problem for schools or teachers themselves. Every year, principals and school systems struggle to replace the teachers who burn out and leave. The National Commission on Teaching and America's Future reports that one-third of new teachers leave after three years, and almost half are gone within five.[4] Rather than dipping deeper into the barrel of potential hires than a principal might wish, and foisting these teachers onto impressionable children, principals and

---

4. National Commission on Teaching and America's Future, *No Dream Denied: A Pledge to America's Children*, 2003, 10, http://nctaf.org/wp-content/uploads/2012/01/no-dream-denied_summary_report.pdf.

school systems could maintain their teams at a smaller size, and focus more resources on the high performers who remain. With good tools, these remaining teachers are likely to be more satisfied.

Some smart philanthropy is betting that this increased teacher satisfaction will be the catalyst that truly spreads blended learning in schools. Already, it is teacher interest that has driven the mass adoption of ed-tech programs such as Class Dojo and EdModo. Money spent introducing teachers to blended learning will thus be money well spent. Over time, the teaching corps will be made up of more and more digital natives who can't imagine teaching without the technology that's ubiquitous in their personal lives.

Roe, who taught for many years using technology, but not in a blended model, says that "it's a new thing to learn how to teach this way. But that makes it interesting. For me, the results prove this is the way to go." In its first year, Summit's new blended-learning model was certainly "a lot more stressful and a lot more work." On the other hand, "it was more enjoyable," says this math teacher. And "we feel it's better for our kids."

Lever 4: Cost Control

Most education money comes from state and local governments. Many states and cities find themselves in dire fiscal straits today, and the public mood is turning toward austerity. One of the major attractions of blended learning is the possibility of eventually getting better results without extra spending, and perhaps even getting better results while spending less than states and cities are now.

Cost control is not easy to achieve in education. While many goods have gotten cheaper over time, education has seen very few productivity gains, and over the last generation has mostly become a lot more expensive per unit of output. The basic structure of education—a teacher standing in front of a group of students—hasn't changed much since the days of Socrates. Meanwhile, many extra expectations have been piled onto schools that require staff, machinery, large physical spaces, and money—everything from busing, to athletic teams, to hot meals, to custodial care for working parents.

There is, however, no reason that education needs to cost as much as Americans are now paying. We pay more per pupil than South Korea, Finland, and other high-performing countries that also provide lots of teachers, modern buildings, and ample books and amenities. Decades of studies by scholars like Stanford economist Eric Hanushek have shown that Americans have gotten very little from the gush of money that has been directed into K–12 education over the last generation.[5]

---

5. See, for instance, Eric A. Hanushek, "The Failure of Input-based Schooling Policies," *Economic Journal*, February 2003, F64–F98, http://www.nber.org/papers/w9040.

> Digital learning doesn't eliminate the need
> for high-quality teaching.

With many states and the federal government now in fiscal crisis amid record spending, K–12 spending in the U.S. will have to become more productive. The tantalizing prospect of blended learning is that it could help states and districts do just that. Ethan Gray, director of the Cities for Education Entrepreneurship Trust (CEE-Trust), a network of city-focused foundations and mayors' offices that support education reform, says, "I don't frame it as lower cost. I frame it as a different business model. . . . The easiest way to put it is it makes good teaching less expensive."

Summit schools head Diane Tavenner identifies the obvious starting point. "If a computer can replace a teacher, it should. We need to identify every single place where a computer can legitimately replace a teacher and replace them there."

"Digital learning doesn't eliminate the need for high-quality teaching," notes Rick Ogston of Carpe Diem. "It emphasizes the need for more, because technology can't do the higher-order instruction."

Technology does eliminate lower-order teaching, though. As a result, "schools can be a lot more selective," suggests Bryan Hassel, "so every student has better teachers on average." And the financial savings "can flow back to teachers in part, so they can earn more. That'll recruit more good teachers in and keep better teachers longer."

One place the substitution of digital learning for low-grade teaching is already starting to happen is in the higher education market. As with K–12 schools, many state universities are suffering from today's government fiscal crisis. But since families pay a portion of higher education costs directly, there is added pressure to cut costs. So some universities are rethinking how college courses should be taught.

Virginia Tech, for instance, now teaches freshman math in a giant computer lab called the "Math Emporium." It is housed in a space that used to be a discount department store. Picture hundreds of students, each sitting at an Apple computer with a red plastic cup next to it.

As described in a *Washington Post* investigation,[6] students work through the freshman math curriculum online. If they get stuck and require help

---

6. Daniel de Vise, "At Virginia Tech, Computers Help Solve a Math Class Problem," *Washington Post*, April 22, 2012, http://www.washingtonpost.com/local/education/at-virginia-tech-computers-help-solve-a-math-class-problem/2012/04/22/gIQAmAOmaT_story.html.

from a human being, they place the red cup on top of their monitor. Circulating teachers (who are not professors) descend to answer questions and help students stay on track.

In many ways, the computers provide a more sure product than you'd get from a grad student who's teaching freshman math as part of his stipend. Traditional lectures give students little chance to actually do math. And lecture classes don't help if a student has a crucial gap in his background knowledge. The result, according to the *Post*, is that Virginia Tech students now pass math classes at a higher rate than they did previously, at a third less cost.

Virginia Tech's experience is not unusual. Recently, education think tank Ithaka S+R assigned over 600 undergraduates to two groups: one that took a traditional introductory statistics course that met in person three hours per week, and one that took a blended-learning course that used an

> Blended learning can lower costs, reducing the fundamental mismatch between the expenses of good education and the resources available in, for instance, inner-city Catholic schools.

online curriculum from Carnegie Mellon supplemented by meetings once per week. Both groups did the same on the final exam.[7] What was different? Students in the blended learning course spent about 25 percent less time on the class, even as they achieved the same results.

Once the start-up costs were accounted for, the Ithaka S+R researchers estimated operating costs of the blended-learning course at about half that of the traditional class—mostly because of lower personnel costs. The downside was that students in the blended-learning version of the statistics class were less satisfied—a downside worth careful consideration in these early years of blended learning when proponents are trying to marshal broad support for the idea. The software didn't have a whole lot of entertaining features, and the right professor can be fun to listen to. Students also appreciate the human element of education, and having ready access to a teacher. With careful design, though, some of those disadvantages

---

7. William G. Bowen et al., "Interactive Learning Online at Public Universities: Evidence from Randomized Trials," Ithaka S+R, May 22, 2012, available online at http://www.sr.ithaka.org/research-publications/interactive-learning-online-public-universities-evidence-randomized-trials

Can Blended Learning Rescue Catholic Schools?

One important branch of American schooling that is extremely interested in the question of financial sustainability is religious schools—particularly Catholic ones. In the U.S. today, there are more than two million students enrolled in Catholic schools, including many living in inner-city neighborhoods whose options, and life course, would be extremely bleak if their Catholic schools were to close. Yet Catholic schools *are* closing, at alarming rates, for simple economic reasons. Back in the 1960s there were more than five million American children in Catholic schools.[1] Few organizations can survive a 50 percent loss of market share.

There are many reasons for that decline, including the disappearance of nuns who provided low-cost teaching, and the seismic residential and demographic shifts that reshaped city neighborhoods over the last generation. The net result is that many students enrolled in Catholic schools—particularly urban Catholic schools—are poor children who can't pay full tuition. And the urban Catholic parishes that subsidize these schools are having difficulty keeping up with costs.

Between 2000 and 2012, 1,942 Catholic schools closed down or consolidated, resulting in a contraction of 24 percent of all available spots. These numbers matter even for Americans who don't use Catholic schools, because those children don't disappear when a school closes. They tend to come into the local public school system, where taxpayers pay for their education. If a school system spends $10,000 per child, then 100 students who transfer out of a closing Catholic school cost the state and local taxpayers a million dollars. And the subsequent trajectory of many of those students may be less positive even with this large spending. Many Catholic schools produce stellar academic outcomes, and some more modest ones, but all tend to be safe places with good discipline and character training, who send higher percentages of their students

---

1. Dale McDonald and Margaret M. Schultz, "United States Catholic Elementary and Secondary Schools, 2011-2012: The Annual Statistical Report on Schools, Enrollment and Staffing," National Catholic Educational Association, available at http://www.ncea. org/news/annualdatareport.asp#full

to college than comparable public schools, and whose students and families tend to be much happier.

A few innovative models have helped Catholic schools with their financial dilemma. The Cristo Rey network began in Chicago and now operates dozens of Catholic schools across the country, with as many more in development (with strong philanthropic support from the likes of the Walton Family Foundation, the Gates Foundation, and the Cassin Educational Initiative Foundation). It employs a very distinctive curriculum that includes placing all students in clerical jobs with local companies. Students work one or two days per week, and companies pay temp wages, which subsidize tuition. As a bonus, children learn about the working world, and what careers await them should they graduate and go to college.

Helpful as that strategy has proven to be, it does not moderate the costs of Catholic education; it merely shifts them to businesses. Blended learning, on the other hand, has the potential to actually lower costs, reducing the fundamental mismatch between the expenses of good Catholic education and the resources that inner-city families and local parishes have available to meet those expenses.

Starting a blended-learning Catholic school is expensive, says Richard Riordan, whose foundation has made technology grants to Catholic schools. "But once they get going, probably in the second or third year, it will save about 30 percent of the costs of operating a school. So that's a good reason for anybody to use it, not just Catholic schools."

Done right, blended-learning programs could also improve academic rigor, even on limited resources. That double win could have crucial effects in making Catholic education, or any religious education, sustainable for a new generation. "If you have a better way of educating kids today, why wouldn't believers want to do it too?" asks Scott Hamilton, co-founder and managing partner of Seton Education Partners, a nonprofit devoted to improving Catholic education.

Consequently, a few Catholic schools are leading the way in testing new models—in part because their financial situation is even more dire than the public schools, and in part because they are not beholden to districts, and so can be nimble and experiment. Seton Education Partners' Phaedrus Initiative brings blended models to Catholic schools. The first pilot school, Mission Dolores Academy in San Francisco, was quite an undertaking. Not only was there no wireless in the building at first, but of the $500,000 Seton invested, a full $12,000 first had to be used to build a working phone system.

Some software worked well for children below grade level, but did a lousy job for those at par, or vice versa. Then there was human variability. "At Mission Dolores we had some grades that did really well academically, and made huge gains in those first few months, and other grades didn't have good gains at all. That requires some analysis," says Hamilton—and some nudging of one teacher to go visit another's classroom and see exactly what she was doing differently.

Over time, though, Mission Dolores was able to lower operating costs while simultaneously boosting achievement. After seeing those results, the Phaedrus Initiative funded a second pilot at St. Therese in Seattle, a K–8 school that opened as a blended-learning institution in fall 2012. In doing so, St. Therese increased its enrollment by more than 50 children while the fixed costs stayed the same, "so economically, it's a win," says Hamilton. "There's so much potential here if we do it right." Seton Education Partners and the Phaedrus Initiative will open five more blended Catholic schools in 2013–2014.

Across the country in North Philadelphia, Visitation School has recently instituted, in addition to its fourth-grade blended pilot described earlier, a blended program for children of all ages who need extra assistance in math. On the first floor of a stately building constructed in the 19th century, Sr. Margaret Duffy shuffles groups of children through her resource room. While she works intensely with two fifth-grade girls on rounding, a young boy adds two- and three-digit numbers on DreamBox.

The children enrolled in these special math intervention classes are "extremely different" in their abilities, notes Sr. Jane Field, the assistant principal. Getting good data on what they know allows you to "get into the brain of the kid," she says. And with the DreamBox software offering the kids practice time and instruction, "this gives Margaret the chance to deal with what they really need"—in a world where there simply aren't resources to hire additional Sr. Margarets.

What Catholic schools are discovering about blended learning is that it's perfectly compatible with any specialty or academic focus a school might have. It's completely ecumenical, which is why other religious schools competing for students with the free public schools may also give it a look. The Avi Chai Foundation, for instance, has funded blended learning in Jewish day schools. A Cristo Rey school, built on the idea of real-world professional experience, could still offer blended learning during academic time.

For that matter, a school with an arts hook, or a health-careers specialty, could also be blended. Blended learning is simply another way of delivering academic content in a more focused and effective fashion. While the Andovers and Exeters of the world might not need to control costs, the promise of efficiency gains is appealing for any private school that needs to serve average-income families. That could be a private school serving middle-class families who feel their children are lost in the shuffle at the local public school, or it could be private schools operating in the developing world.[2] So in a great

many places where cost-control is important, blended learning could be a blessing.

---

show up at school one day out of every five in Bangladesh, Indonesia, Ecuador and Peru, and one day out of four in India and Uganda. Another study found that the teachers in India who did show up spent less than half their time actually instructing children. If parents in these places want their children to receive any education at all, they are often paying tutors or for-profit operators. With that inherent demand, there are plenty of incentives for schools to spring up providing low-cost, tech-based private education. In his book, *The One World Schoolhouse*, Sal Khan notes that inexpensive tablet computers entering the Indian market cost about $100. If a device lasts five years, the annual cost is $20. Khan Academy lessons, meanwhile, are free, and "designed so that students can get what they need in one to two hours a day of following lessons and working out problems; this means that a single tablet could be used by four to as many as 10 students a day." Obviously, there's the matter of internet access, but "bandwidth-hogging videos can be preloaded on devices and user data could be transmitted over cellular networks," Khan suggests.

---

2. A World Bank survey done in 2002 and 2003 found that teachers didn't even

can be eliminated or compensated for. Schools can arrange more face-to-face meetings, and choose software that's more witty and humane.

And, of course, it's important to remember that the status quo isn't perfect either. While the traditional class members in this particular case may have enjoyed themselves, listening to a different professor might have been torture. And even if the students found the blended-learning program less enjoyable, it gave them a lot of extra free hours to have fun in other ways, thanks to that 25 percent time saving. Consuming less time and less money for the same results may justify some trade-offs in a world where the cost of tuition, room, and board at a four-year public college has risen 42 percent after inflation in just the last decade.

Top universities like Carnegie Mellon, Harvard, Stanford, and MIT are developing detailed online courses covering many of the basic subjects college students take. Since class size isn't limited to the fire-code capacity of a lecture hall, thousands of students can enroll in what are starting to be called "MOOCs"—massive open online courses. One possibility is that other colleges will outsource the basic presentation of material to these online courses, and deploy their own educators to focus on small-group instruction. If some of these educators needn't be tenured professors, the cost savings could be large. This change would involve separating the teaching and research functions at universities, but in many cases that has already happened, with full professors spending relatively little time on the teaching of undergraduates.

Some K–12 blended schools are also starting to see productivity gains. Rocketship schools, as we saw earlier, have up to now been able to generate 15 percent margins on standard per-pupil allotments—which they then plow into opening new schools, training teachers, and other priorities. Carpe Diem is likewise financially sustainable because of its 75-to-1 pupil-to-teacher ratio. Educators at KIPP Empower Academy in Los Angeles adopted a blended model to make the most of the increased class sizes that California's student funding cuts necessitated.

Purchasing computers and software to start a blended-learning school is expensive. Many foundations have paid for planning grants and for consultants to help schools select software and design their programs. This start-up capital has been extremely helpful for these schools, though it raises concerns about scalability. Philanthropists won't be able to give start-up funds to all schools serving 50 million American children.

The good news is that planning becomes less complicated with each passing year. One of the projects of the Learning Accelerator, the philanthropy-seeded organization that aims to ease the set-up of blended-learning operations in school districts, will be to create a partially standardized package for launching a blended-learning school. "We'll have arrived at some basic standards, some basic protocols on what a good implementation looks like," says investor Joe Wolf, who is one of the project's backers. That way, consulting work can be "a $30,000 project rather than a $300,000 project."

On the hardware front, some schools might have a "BYOD" policy: bring your own device. College students bring laptops to class; in some places K–12 students are also expected to acquire a computer, sometimes with help from revolving loan funds or group-discount options. Philanthropists could make more targeted investments for families who can't afford technology, versus the majority who (given the market penetration of smartphones and laptops) clearly can.

Another bit of good news on costs is that even students who live close to the poverty line have more access to technology than people assume. When Harsh Patel decided to experiment with Khan Academy in his Chicago classroom, he rounded up as many computers as possible from donations and arranged ways for kids to use the computers after hours. But he soon learned that about 80 percent of his students had access to the internet in some form at home. Meanwhile, tablet and laptop prices are falling rapidly; at $200, purchasing a new machine for each student can be cost-competitive with the usual budget for textbooks and photocopying.

There are still reasons why blended-learning schools might not see immediate productivity gains. Software costs money, as does teacher time as educators figure out new ways of working. If schools need to employ a technology specialist, this eats up some of the savings gained by bigger class sizes. And if you don't adopt bigger class sizes, you won't see any cost savings at all.

There is, however, good reason to expect that blended learning could eventually help schools function well even on reduced per-pupil allocations. If they can produce good results on less than existing funding allotments, they'll be able to use leftover funds for the extras that attract parents and students: art, music, field trips, even nicer school buildings to match all their brand-new technology.

Barriers to the Growth of Blended Learning

If existing blended-learning schools are getting good results, why hasn't the practice spread more widely? One obvious answer is that the current schools are very new. Hardly any have more than just a few years of experience. Moreover, starting a new school—or radically transforming an older school's structure—is a complicated undertaking that is not for the faint of heart.

Merit Prep in Newark opened its doors in August 2012 as one of New Jersey's first two schools blending in-person and online instruction. Founder Ben Rayer has his work cut out for him: While a sign on the green-accented walls of this school across from City Hall says, "To mastery and beyond," the beginning reality is that just 17 percent of his 80 new sixth-grade students are performing at grade level.

The office building the school is occupying already had a wide central space (Merit Prep teachers and students call it "the stadium"), so there were few architectural difficulties in getting the facility up and running around a computer-filled core. A more serious existential challenge threatened this new charter school, though: a suit from the state teachers union, known as the New Jersey Education Association, asking for an injunction that would prevent the school even from opening. Their argument was that New Jersey's Department of Education lacked the authority to authorize online charter schools—even though Merit Prep's students are most emphatically in a school building, and learning from flesh and blood teachers, a scenario that has little in common with the virtual schools operating in several other states.

A judge denied the union's motion, but did so without ruling on the merits of the suit, which will grind forward over the next year, a cloud over this burst of idealism. Needless to say, the possibility of facing a major lawsuit from opponents of new methods can dampen enthusiasm for starting new styles of schools. And that's not the only obstacle standing in the way of more blended-learning experiments. Here are a few other major reasons why blended learning is not yet available on a large scale.

Bottleneck 1: A Lack of Research

While blended-learning proponents can point to some initially good test scores, there is little solid data published in peer-reviewed journals. "Honestly, it's so early on, no one knows what works and doesn't work," says Diane Tavenner, leader of Summit Public Schools. "Indeed," notes Scott Benson, who directs blended-learning grants at the Bill & Melinda Gates Foundation, "part of me is really nervous—that the dialogue and enthusiasm is outpacing the results."

Education involves humans, and human outcomes are affected by so many variables that it's hard to pin any result to one thing. The fact that one teacher got good test results in a blended classroom may mean that blended learning worked. Or it may mean that you had a great teacher who was willing to try new things. It sounds impressive to know that at KIPP Empower Academy, the kindergartners went from 64 percent basic or below basic achievement on the STEP literacy assessment to just 4 percent basic or below basic, and 96 percent proficient or advanced. It also sounds good that in the Khan Academy Los Altos pilot, twice as many seventh-grade students in developmental math were at grade level at the end of the year as at the beginning. Yet you can't assert that any other school that tries the same thing will get the same results.

One ongoing project in blended learning is to gather more good data. Cheryl Niehaus, an education program officer at the Michael & Susan Dell Foundation who follows blended learning closely, says, "Last year, one thing stood out: how much activity there was, how much excitement. And also how relatively little information there is on what works for students in a blended-learning model." To help address this, Dell commissioned its five white papers on blended learning schools (please see chapter 3) and a study from the Stanford Research Institute on quantitative results from those schools.

There are a few pieces of sophisticated evidence. One meta-analysis of blended-learning studies[1] looked at research published between 1996 and 2008 that met minimum quality standards. The results were mixed, but 11 of the 51 studies favored online or blended learning, while two favored face-to-face education.

Brian Greenberg who was the chief academic officer of Envision Schools before joining the Silicon Schools Fund, ran a study comparing blended learning and traditional instruction in a five-week summer-school program in Oakland for students who had failed algebra. The same teacher taught both sections, and children were randomly assigned to the blended-learning class or a traditional class. At the end of the program, the children from the blended-learning section showed slightly more improvement from their pre-test to their post-test. "The gains themselves were not particularly robust," says Greenberg, but what was interesting is that the test was a "pure algebra measure." Many of the kids in the blended learning section "spent a good portion of their summer on pre-algebra skills," as the data quickly revealed that they had all sorts of gaps in their pre-algebra math knowledge, which may have been why they failed algebra in the first place. The value of filling in those gaps "doesn't come up if you're only testing algebra," but it should show itself in other math work by those students. Greenberg's summary is that the blended kids "spent less time on algebra than the regular kids, yet did as well or better" on an algebra assessment. Based on that result, he's since been working on rolling out broader blended-learning programs, most notably in all the schools launched by the Silicon Schools Fund, a fund financed by the Fisher Fund and other donors to start blended schools in the San Francisco Bay area.

1. U. S. Department of Education, "Evaluation of Evidence-Based Practices in Online Learning: A Meta-Analysis and Review of Online Learning Studies," September 2010, http://www2.ed.gov/rschstat/eval/tech/evidence-based-practices/finalreport.pdf.

For its remedial math class, Arizona State University in 2011 launched a pilot using Knewton, an adaptive learning software platform. According to Knewton COO David Liu, withdrawal rates dropped by 56 percent, pass rates increased, and 45 percent of the students finished the class early. That last statistic hadn't been kept before, because it wasn't possible until the daily assessment and instant dashboard postings of the blended model made it possible to know when individual students had reached mastery. Given that long stints in remedial classes can lessen the chance that a student finishes college, anything that speeds the process along could have outsized results.

In the long run, this ability of instructors to see specific things in individual student performance that were invisible before will be one of blended learning's greatest assets. A few weeks before California's statewide assessments, Juan Nuñez at Thurgood Marshall learned, thanks to the constant streams of data he was receiving from his computer programs, that his students were struggling with two skills that were going to be tested. Looking back, he could see that these skills hadn't been covered adequately in the curriculum. So he decided,

> Blended learning is founded on data and measurement. Over time, the measures will get richer. Given the initial results, proponents are bullish.

"let me take this week to go ahead and teach that explicitly." Without the feedback that his students didn't know those skills, he wouldn't have gone back to fill that gap, and his students' understanding and performance outcomes would have been lower.

Even if there isn't yet much official overarching data on what works, the first bit of good news is that multiple new studies are in process right now, with many of the results due in 2013. Financing research can be a philanthropic sweet spot since it is an area that people busy running schools tend to underinvest in. The field of education spends shockingly small portions of overall budget on R&D—by some measures, less than 1 percent (compared to double digits in the pharmaceutical industry, for instance). One result of that discrepancy is that while a doctor facing a common condition—perhaps childhood asthma—is starting to have a well-tested protocol of treatment to apply, educators facing similarly common conditions do not. Philanthropists can help put funds where education policymakers have failed to.

A final bit of good news is that blended learning is itself founded on data and measurement, so its practitioners are able to make good decisions about efficacy long before they see the results of complex multi-year double-blind studies. Over time, the statistical measures will get richer. And given the initial results, blended-learning proponents are bullish.

Bottleneck 2: The *Dilbert* Reaction

Another bottleneck slowing blended learning has to do with what it looks like compared to the archetypal vision of education, or at least education as grown-ups wax nostalgic about it. "There's a lot of 'small c' conservatism" among parents and educators, says Michael Horn of the Innosight Institute. They say, "This is how I went to school. Why shouldn't my kids have the same experience?"

Even people who like the idea of technology in schools can have a visceral reaction to pictures of children sitting in what looks like a cubicle farm in Scott Adams' *Dilbert* comic strip. Grown-ups don't like logging time in cubicles, so why would they want that for their children? Even some tech titans resist that for their children. An October 2011 story in the *New York Times* described a Waldorf School in Silicon Valley—which attracts offspring of people like the chief technology officer of eBay—where screens are not allowed in the classroom, and educators believe that "computers inhibit creative thinking, movement, human interaction, and attention spans."[2]

We all have romantic notions of what education looks like, often involving wooden desks, dusty books, a chalkboard, and a teacher in a houndstooth blazer. Blended learning doesn't look like that. High pupil-to-teacher ratios are also jarring for parents who have had the idea drummed into them that smaller classes must be better. "No laptop can replace a teacher" is a common refrain that captures this visceral reaction.

While it is certainly true that computers and teachers are far from interchangeable, we live in an era that increasingly differentiates between the core aspects of a job and the peripheral elements. Robots weld car frames, while humans adjust door fits. Computers collect basic information, then customer-service reps swoop in to answer questions on what insurance policy is right for you.

A laptop most definitely can replace a teacher when it comes to taking attendance, grading quizzes, conducting performance assessments, and presenting basic content. If a teacher doesn't have to spend time on these things,

---

2. Matt Richtel, "At Waldorf School in Silicon Valley, Technology Can Wait," *New York Times*, October 22, 2011, http://www.nytimes.com/2011/10/23/technology/at-waldorf-school-in-silicon-valley-technology-can-wait.html.

she can focus, instead, on what might actually be her core capabilities: helping children learn how to learn, and inspiring them to keep at it. It is this extra teacher time and attention that proponents of blended learning find parents most need to see to believe. Providing visual evidence of these schools working is one reason the Jaquelin Hume Foundation funded the creation of videos of several blended-learning institutions, and brings journalists, legislators, and community leaders on site visits to see the classrooms for themselves. City-Bridge Foundation's Education Innovation Fellowship likewise brings teachers to blended classrooms so they can observe this individualized attention first hand. When parents do see it—even parents who aren't sending their kids to failing schools—many are quite intrigued.

The evolution of computers into more intimate and responsive forms may help with this initial distrust. The rise of tablet computers and very cheap laptops that kids can curl up with in reading nooks may ease some of the visceral reaction against seeing kids lined up in regimented rows of monitors. Lots of laptops sprawled across classroom tables looks like your average Starbucks, rather than a cube farm.

Moreover: the Silicon Valley titans who send their children to a screen-less Waldorf-style school are able to train their children in modern technology in lots of other ways. Lower-income parents may be much more anxious for their children to learn in school the skills necessary for success in the modern economy. "I was a little bit surprised at how much blended learning appealed to poor minority parents in San Francisco," says Scott Hamilton of Seton Education Partners. "They're not well versed in digital learning and curricular offerings, but they know that computers are central to their children's employability and life as adults."

As for the changing role of teachers, "The feeling I have as a parent is I'm absolutely not willing to relinquish that teacher connection. Teacher as a mentor, teacher as a guide—that's totally crucial, almost more than ever," says Heather Staker, whose children attend Acton Academy in Austin. But with online instruction in core subjects freeing up teacher time, her children get more teacher attention, and get to learn how they learn best. "It's been exciting to see my own kids find their passions," she says. One daughter discovered she's got a knack for math and is now soaring ahead. "I don't think she would be unleashed that way in a traditional environment," Staker says. That's worth letting go of nostalgic fantasies of chalkboards and dusty textbooks.

Bottleneck 3: Misguided Policy
Education policy is often the object of a tug-of-war among different inter-

> Many of blended learning's first adopters have been charter schools, simply because blended instruction requires fresh and flexible thinking.

est groups. Scads of local, state, and federal policies create obstacles for blended learning, even when that's not the explicit intention. Many of blended learning's first adopters have been charter schools rather than traditional district-run schools, simply because blended instruction requires fresh and flexible thinking among administrators and teachers, and that is more common at charters. But even within the charter-school sector there are serious legal and administrative obstacles:

- Some states have limits on the overall number of charter schools that block further growth.

- Some states regulate charter schools in ways that inhibit innovation, such as blocking for-profit operators or cyber charters, and demanding particular teacher-to-student ratios, even in online schools.

- Many charter schools receive far less than the amount of funding given to their district counterparts.

- Some states don't adequately assess charter schools, allowing low-quality operations to undermine support for more rigorous institutions. ("We let a thousand flowers bloom," says Gisèle Huff of the Hume Foundation, "and half of them were weeds.")

Even policies that sound quite reasonable can thwart deeper thinking about education, and may limit the growth of blended learning over time. Take rules on class sizes. According to Bryan Hassel of Public Impact, 36 states have some sort of limit on class size. These rules seem well-intentioned, but they create two problems. First, they apply equally to all teachers, regardless of quality, even though 28 students assigned to a teacher in the top quartile will likely do better than 22 students assigned to a teacher in the bottom quartile. Second, if you can't increase class sizes, then blended-learning programs are doomed to remain small and uneconomic. If you have all the start-up costs associated with the technology but can't capture the productivity and quality gains associated with increased class sizes led by a smaller universe of superior teachers, then you'll just have more expensive schools, not better ones.

The list of policies made for a different era goes on and on. Teacher licensing requirements can inhibit blended schools. Some union contracts present intractable obstacles to advanced digital learning. State textbook procurement processes often make no sense when content can be delivered digitally and updated constantly. Annual tests whose results are delivered far too late to actually affect instruction can just waste time in a universe where students are assessed constantly.

Susan Patrick of iNACOL says, "A huge focus of our time is on policy—policymakers asking us what are the barriers in my state. It's nice that we're a membership association so we can reach out to both schools and school districts and ask 'What are you facing as barriers? What's really happening?'"

Perhaps the most reasonable-sounding but misguided policy is that in many states, school funding is based on kids spending a certain number of hours and days at school (e.g., six hours a day for 180 days). This makes sense for ensuring a standard amount of instruction time. But this "seat time" concept is a blunt instrument for measuring learning. A school that has children passively watching TV each week is compensated the same as a school that manages to move children through and above grade levels in a lesser amount of time.

"I'm convinced that key elements of online and blended learning cannot thrive under the constraints of today's systems of education governance, finance, and choice," says Chester E. Finn Jr., president of the Thomas B. Fordham Foundation. "This technology has the potential to revolutionize the entire education delivery system—but the system has plenty of vested interests that will do all in their power to keep that from happening."

Education isn't the only field that has struggled with counterproductive public policy. In medicine, payers have for many years compensated providers for procedures carried out, rather than paying for good results. A hospital with a high rate of re-admittance due to complications has been able to bill more than a hospital that gets people home quickly and keeps them there. This creates few incentives for quality care.

Imagining different ways of compensating schools is fascinating. Would it be possible to reimburse partly based on mastery? On how much students improve compared to their starting point? What would school look like if the knowledge necessary to be a high-school graduate—or even to complete a particular grade—was broken down into specific units, and then students needed to demonstrate that they had accomplished each one? Any organization that moved the student to mastery, whether in the 1,080 hours students usually sit in chairs each year, or in more time or less, could be paid for accomplishing that.

A broader funding question is how online course providers should be compensated. In current blended-learning models, schools generally select software to be offered school-wide, and purchase it out of school funds. What about when students take pure online courses that feature teachers located elsewhere? Some policies make even this partial adoption of technology difficult. In California, notes Patrick, students can only enroll in online courses offered by neighboring districts—as if the internet doesn't work over long distances.

Some districts are willing to pay an online provider for a course the school doesn't offer itself. That raises another interesting question. What if a school does offer a course, yet students or parents want to enroll in an online alternative?

Well-developed online learning introduces possibilities of "school choice" on a course-by-course basis. The most enlightened idea would be for funding to follow the child wherever she goes, right down to the individual course level. A portion of the child's education allotment from the state could go to the online operator, and a portion might also go to the bricks-and-mortar school where the child is sitting, to cover the cost of their utilities, adult supervision, and so forth. Good policies are clearly possible, if political and regulatory obstacles can be surmounted.

The process of figuring all this out is going to slow the adoption of digital and blended learning. Some states, though, are trying innovative approaches. In 2005, New Hampshire became the first state to eliminate the Carnegie unit (the standard time-based measurement for learning). New Hampshire now requires schools to grant high-school credit based on competency rather than seat time.

Philanthropists can play a big role in changing misguided policies. Foundations including the Hume Foundation, the Gates Foundation, and others have supported iNACOL. Others have supported the Foundation for Excellence in Education (run by former Florida Gov. Jeb Bush) and the Alliance for Excellent Education (run by former West Virginia Gov. Bob Wise). Together, the two former governors chair Digital Learning Now, an organization that advocates for sensible digital-learning policies.

Well-developed online learning introduces possibilities of "school choice" on a course-by-course basis.

Frequently, says Wise, what's needed most is "clearing out the underbrush" of policies that no longer make sense. "Often, legislatures don't do technology well. In the time it takes to reach a compromise, the technology has already advanced two to three generations." Wise warns that "the decisions made in the next two years will set up education for the next two decades." To encourage good policies, Digital Learning Now rates states based on how they compare to their peers. Over time, sunlight and public exposure of this sort could alter policies that discourage 21st-century learning.

Bottleneck 4: Inertia

Perhaps the biggest barrier to the growth of blended learning is that public education by nature tends to be glacial in its rate of movement and change. The hundreds of billions of dollars spent nationally on public schools have created entrenched lobbies dedicated to protecting the status quo. More neutrally, schools are the heart of many communities, and they have long traditions that people naturally protect. Sometimes educational innovation is great, but often it is just faddish. Says Michael Horn of the Innosight Institute, "There are a lot of people jumping in and doing blended learning because it's the cool thing to do right now, without giving a lot of thought to why or what problem they're solving." A bad precedent could sour the movement quickly.

So, plenty of schools cling to a "wait-and-see" kind of attitude. That can be frustrating—particularly given the complacency that causes many communities to imagine their local schools are just fine, even while they recognize that the national averages are profoundly mediocre. "Parents sometimes see the flowers blooming around the flagpole out front and the new team uniforms and assume, 'Man, our school must be kicking it!' But they're missing what's important," warns former Arizona schools head Lisa Keegan.

If the point of schools is to produce great educational outcomes for students, then many of today's public institutions have deep, systematic inadequacies. On the other hand, if you view big school systems as job programs for adults in the community, as places to keep kids quiet and safe during custodial periods while parents work, then most are doing fine, and any change to established means of operation—particularly one involving fewer jobs and more accountability, which might eventually be the case with blended learning—is likely to be treated as an existential threat.

Joe Williams, the head of Democrats for Education Reform, says that within teacher unions "the slippery slope argument comes up. If you allow students to start taking classes online without being in a school, at some point you'll have fewer teachers—so this is the end of the world."

Merit Badges

How do the Boy Scouts know a young man has mastered the science of first aid? The organization grants him a merit badge when he's demonstrated competence in certain skills. He can display the badge proudly, and all other scouts know what it means: this boy can dress your wounds in a jiffy.

The idea of "micro-credentialing"—a fancy word for merit badges—is gaining steam in education. The bachelor's degree, for instance, shows that you've attended and passed a certain number of classes, but it doesn't necessarily indicate mastery of any particular skill *per se*, in a way that's standardized across universities. Employers staring at a pile of résumés find it difficult to figure out just on the basis of a bachelor's degree who will make a good employee. The tendency is consequently to hire people who've completed internships (often unpaid), who have gone to brand-name schools, or whose relatives and friends already work for that employer. None of this advances the cause of equity or a competitive labor market.

Merit badges could fill that gap. The John D. and Catherine T. MacArthur Foundation sponsored a contest in 2012, along with software-maker Mozilla, to come up with digital badges for particular skills that organizations want to assess. Sal Khan reports that the Khan Academy is working on a merit badge for college algebra and one for remedial (or "developmental") math. "Students don't like having to pay tuition to take developmental math," he says, so brushing up with Khan Academy and then being able to demonstrate mastery could be a way around an otherwise costly requirement.

Mastery-based credentialing fits well in the world of information technology, says Khan. The computer-programming industry already is almost ignoring credentials like college degrees and asking candidates instead "What can you do?" Khan says he is surprised that no one has come up with a truly credible micro-credentialing system before now. "The old way of assessing is just broken," he says. Any time he talks about merit badges, "almost everyone gives these huge nods of approval."

Reform, he notes, "is a lot more difficult than I ever imagined. There's still a clock-punching mentality."

Sometimes it takes a literal act of God—as happened when much of New Orleans was wiped off the map during Hurricane Katrina in 2005—to up-end the status quo. With many schools under water, reformers came in and started opening new programs within days. Now, more than 80 percent of New Orleans children attend charter schools, some of which—like FirstLine schools—are experimenting with blended learning. Test scores are slowly rising. With this level of charter market share, actual market discipline is rearing its head, and the state board of education is forcing ineffective schools to close.

Though change is hard, philanthropists who work with younger teachers believe that generational change will aid progress in this area. Williams notes that "there are groups of younger teachers who are willing to keep their minds open for these kinds of changes." Technology itself is neutral, and plenty of teachers now earn their own master's degrees through what are, in essence, blended-learning programs.

Young teachers who want their elementary-school charges to hear a song will naturally pull up YouTube to find it. Internet access "is water to them," says Caprice Young of the Laura and John Arnold Foundation. So the battles of today may not be the battles of tomorrow. The American Federation of Teachers, for instance, is working on creating a national program that would help teachers share lesson plans based on the emerging Common Core standards, recognizing how technology can make teachers much more effective. "The union leadership wants to find ways to be relevant with younger teachers," says Williams.

Philanthropists who would like to be helpful in this process need to find ways to work with anyone interested in using technology to improve student outcomes, even if they have other disagreements. Building broad, democratic support for digital forms of learning is essential. Says Alex Hernandez of the Charter School Growth Fund: "Where we've seen innovation really take off is where there's been a well-developed ecosystem of folks who want to innovate and people who want to support them. . . . Unless there's a community of people excited about a reform, change just turns into a mandate, and mandates never work out."

How Innovation Happens

Implementing any new technology that disturbs deep-rooted social structures is tough, and looking at the process at any moment in time is no guarantee you'll see the next step. You have to weave between two extremes: unfounded hype on the one hand, and at the other pole a short-sighted vision that can't see past the way things are now to the way things might be.

Education technology, up to this point, has
not lived up to its promise. Is that changing?

Blended learning has certainly gotten its share of breathless attention. People are desperate for ideas that work in education. Yet "there is a very long and storied track record of education technology, up to this point, not living up to its promise," notes Scott Benson of the Bill & Melinda Gates Foundation. Funders should know that even a well-designed blended-learning program won't quickly bring children failed by their traditional schools up to grade level, mastery, and beyond. "Technology is an amazing tool—it really is—but it's just a tool and if it's not used by good teachers in a strong school culture, it's not going to achieve what a philanthropist would want it to achieve," says Scott Hamilton of Seton Education Partners.

Of course, the flip side of this caution—dismissing blended learning as yet another fad that will be tried and abandoned, much as a kid loses interest in a fading video game—is a flawed approach too. Many people who looked at the internet in the mid-1990s wondered what the fuss was about. As new ideas emerge, it's often hard to see exactly what they might be useful for, or why existing patterns might change.

This stuck-in-time vision has tinted some of the criticism of online and blended learning. When the world started paying attention to Sal Khan's videos, several educators accurately pointed out that lectures—whether online or not—were not a particularly innovative approach to education. One of Khan's most thoughtful critics is Frank Noschese, an award-winning physics teacher at John Jay High School in New York. Noschese blogs about education, and describes how his students learn physics principles through experimentation: using little battery-powered buggies, rulers, and stopwatches to answer that classic physics question about when two trains leaving distant stations would meet. In a good classroom, Noschese has argued, "there's a lot going on that I don't think I can get from a video."[1]

There's also plenty of evidence that expository lectures and problem sets often work poorly. Millions of us studied trigonometry via this method, and promptly forgot everything after the last test. The educational theory of constructivism—advanced by Jean Piaget and others, and dominant in schools of education—holds that people construct knowledge from

---

1. Laura Vanderkam, "The Math of Khan," *City Journal*, Winter 2012.

their experiences and what they care about. While this is often caricatured as children discovering the quadratic equation as they skip through fields of flowers, proponents are not wrong that we tend to absorb and retain deeply things that we figure out on our own, partly because we have personal reasons for wanting to understand. People who hated high-school chemistry figure out acids and bases as they balance the pH of their lawns or gardens. Project learning, done right, is likewise more compelling than videos or online or in-person problem sets.

But the beauty of blended learning is that you can get the best of both worlds. Appropriate technology can expand the reach of a teacher who does an amazing job at presenting material. It can also free up teachers who work best one-on-one so they have more opportunities to ply that skill. Small-group projects that neither bore nor frustrate—and that are aimed at discovery—are much likelier when teachers know exactly what their students have already grasped, and what they are missing (as blended learning promises to reveal more effectively than any class-wide method).

The Achilles' heel of blended learning in its nascent state is that the rich content which is possible hasn't yet been created on the scale that educators dream of. In interviews for this book, person after person complained about gaps and inadequacies in the technology that is currently available. "There isn't really a pure model today. If there was, everybody would be using it," notes Anthony Kim, head of Education Elements, a firm that helps schools select blended-learning software.

The thin supply of programs frustrates attempts to show what blended learning can do, in much the same way that YouTube didn't bloom until most people had broadband access. The blended-learning Holy Grail is software that is adaptive to the student, able to instantly feed rich data back to teachers in useable forms, and exemplary in its subject area, not just part of a common suite. None of the schools profiled in this book yet have technology that meets all those standards.

Jelena Dobic of KIPP says that in L.A.'s Empower Academy, "right now we're not even looking at the data" from the online work students do, because it has not yet proved useful enough for teachers to be able to quickly scan it and decide what the next action should be.

Appropriate technology can expand the reach of a good teacher.

Nonetheless, there is enough solid digital content out there to get schools going and proceed with the process of improvement. Pioneering schools like those profiled in this guidebook are working on overcoming these challenges. Many have collaborative relationships with content providers to test and expand different approaches. They also vote with their dollars; KIPP Empower Academy, for instance, has changed its software to achieve improved analytics.

Kim rates today's content at five on a 10-point scale, and expects rapid progress in the future. "There are a lot of people working on it," he says. Software gets better, as software is wont to do. There is no comparison between the graphics of World of Warcraft today versus the 1990 version of SimCity.

The adoption of disruptive technology is always messy. As Clayton Christensen wrote in *The Innovator's Dilemma*, since new technology tends, at first, to be not especially good, it colonizes the margins of an industry. Right now, educational software is often inferior to the best teachers. But teachers aren't improving at nearly the rate that software is.

There is a lot of venture capital pouring into educational technology. In 2005, venture capitalists put only $13 million into education ventures; by 2011 that was up to $389 million. Deb Quazzo, founder of GSV Advisors, which invests in educational products, set out to discover whether a lack of capital was inhibiting innovation in education. Her answer? "Absolutely not." While it's easy to complain that there isn't enough investment, she challenges observers to name an excellent company that hasn't been funded.

The field is now ramping up rapidly. The NewSchools Venture Fund has seed-funded a host of new entities, including LearnZillion (providing free online lessons for teachers and students), Matchbook Learning (a school operator), and GoalBook (software to manage special education students). "Our approach is to invest relatively small amounts of capital ($50,000-$300,000) in the most promising ed-tech ventures," says Jennifer Carolan of NewSchools Venture Fund. "We then help our companies raise their next round of financing from other capital sources."

The incubator Imagine K–12 has kicked off such companies as Chalk (which simplifies the tsunami of paperwork teachers and schools manage), NoRedInk (which covers grammar), and Tioki (a LinkedIn of sorts for educators). Reasoning Mind, the successful blended program pushed by philanthropists Ernie Cockrell and Forrest Hoglund for teaching math, now has dozens of philanthropic and corporate backers financing its introduction into schools. Over time, products from major players like Knewton, Junyo, DreamBox, Education 2020, Khan Academy, Edmodo, Achieve

> Right now, educational software is often inferior to the best teachers. But teachers aren't improving at nearly the rate that software is.

3000, Revolution K12, and others will continue to get better and more comprehensive. Jessie Woolley-Wilson of DreamBox describes her product as "an adaptive engine." "We're going to continue to grow," she says. "We have not realized our company mission if we limit it to early math."

Meanwhile, good outcomes are possible even with rudimentary tools. "Let's cut them some slack here and look at the results," says Gisèle Huff of the Jaquelin Hume Foundation. "Never mind the glitches, look at the results in spite of that." Education software customers, she says, "are getting 200 percent more than they ever have before, and now they want 500 percent." Over time, a competitive market in content will likely give schools what they want.

The question is which schools will be bold enough to grab hold of the new technology. "Innovation will not come from a rank-and-file district, rank-and-file school, rank-and-file teacher," predicts Brian Greenberg, CEO of the Silicon Schools Fund. "I think we need some sort of beacon schools to go first and show the way."

The Philanthropist's Guide to Smart Investments

Even with the barriers to growth and lingering issues described in the previous chapter, blended learning is expanding. "We're going to start to see a lot more successes in the next year," says Michael Horn of the Innosight Institute. In *Disrupting Class*, the authors predicted that 25 percent of American students would rely on some form of online learning by 2014, and 50 percent by 2019. Already, some ed-tech products like ClassDoJo and EdModo are being deployed in more than 100,000 classrooms. DreamBox experienced 300 percent growth last year—some of that from parents purchasing the product, the rest from schools. A

> Most districts around the country have
> implemented at least some online learning
> in the last two years.

handful of states (Florida, North Carolina, and New Hampshire) now have over a quarter of their students taking online classes either in school or at home. There's nothing stopping the practice from spreading in other states. "Most districts around the country have implemented at least some online learning in the last two years," reports education author Tom Vander Ark. While "in most cases, it's fairly lame," even remedial classes offered over the summer for credit recovery amount to something. "It matters that half of all districts are at least in the game," he says.

States have committed to shifting their annual assessments from pencil-and-paper fill-in-the-circle tests to online examinations by 2014. This means that schools will need computer access for nearly all their students, as well as teachers and school leaders capable of supporting online work. That may create a tipping point that opens the path to wider integration of computers into regular instruction. "My hope is that people don't just buy technology to implement assessments," says former West Virginia Gov. Bob Wise. "Digital learning to us is not just about online learning. It's a total technology strategy. It's about how you're using data systems to inform teachers, how you use adaptive software, about how to use technology to assist teachers. It's about a total comprehensive approach."

Foundations, likewise, are seeing more interest in blended learning from the institutions they support. Jim Blew of the Walton Family Foundation says, "Everybody's doing this now. If we did 150 school start-up grants last year, I bet that 120 of them were using blended learning of some kind." He attributes that development to two things. First, the quest for cost savings in the face of flat revenues, and, second, "the market has begun to mature. Some products clearly help with instruction. Four to five years ago, this was very speculative stuff."

As the blended-learning market matures, philanthropy can play a role in making sure that programs are done thoughtfully and to a high quality standard. Philanthropists can speed adoption via strategic grants. They can make sure that experiments are implemented broadly enough to benefit significant numbers of children.

So how should you invest?

The answer obviously depends on your objectives, your risk tolerance and—not a small matter—what the funder finds most meaningful. The Philanthropy Roundtable surveyed nonprofits, foundations, individual donors, and education-reform leaders about wise giving strategies. Here are some of their ideas for investing at different levels.

Giving In the Under-$100,000 Range

While blended learning is spreading as an educational strategy, many parties who could be champions don't yet know what it is or what it looks like. Thus, many strategies for smaller grants could involve simply raising awareness.

- Convene a summit of local educators and policy makers, and bring in a speaker from a blended-learning school or an organization that works with blended-learning schools. The Donnell-Kay Foundation in Colorado has followed this strategy, producing short conferences over the last three years on blended-learning topics.

- Create a speaker series for the public, bringing experts on blended learning to your town. People who can't attend a multi-day conference might devote an evening to the topic.

- Arrange a trip for local stakeholders to visit blended-learning schools and see for themselves how blended-learning works in practice.

- In an existing or new blended-learning school, offer "professional development" funds that will support the re-training of teachers in the fine points of digital instruction, to ensure the venture has every chance to succeed.

- Create a blended-learning Teacher of the Year award to showcase and reward innovative educators. A Principal of the Year award could do the same thing.

- Support a blended-learning blog or website, which could be either locally or nationally focused. In a national site, guidance on new developments and frank assessments of what is and isn't working in blended learning would be useful. A local site might examine the relevance of blended learning for your particular community, and examine local obstacles and opportunities.

- Pay for outreach and publicity for a successful blended-learning program in your region. The Jaquelin Hume Foundation supported videos for several blended-learning schools (such as Carpe Diem) in order to spread awareness of their models. Better understanding of the practices in actual working schools can elevate the quality of debate.

- Produce a small educational summit for journalists or education bloggers with a focus on blended learning.

- Introduce leaders in other educational organizations, such as PTAs and charter organizations, to blended learning through a conference or site visits.

- Fund more case studies of successful blended-learning schools. The Michael & Susan Dell Foundation has taken this approach with several schools, including the Summit schools, Rocketship, and ATAMS. These case studies can then be circulated nationally to other interested parties beyond those able to make site visits.

- Fund papers, brochures, infographics, and videos on blended learning in general—not specific to particular schools.

- Fund a social-media strategy that raises the profile of blended-learning school leaders and advocates, with the goal of getting these advocates invited to speak to large general audiences (e.g. TED talks) or to make media appearances. A good social-media strategy could generate a community of people who care about blended learning and follow its developments regularly.

- Launch a website for disseminating blended-learning research results more quickly and less expensively than the laborious process followed by peer-reviewed journals.

- Create a meta-analysis of blended-learning research (a review of all the individual studies that have been done). The only existing analysis of this sort was done in 2009 by a bureau of the U.S. Department of Education, and is quickly becoming out of date.

- Fund a smaller research project by a professor or think tank looking at some important detail of digital learning.

- Build a tracking system to provide funders with access to a list of blended-learning projects, how they were funded, and the results.

Encourage fellow philanthropists to use these findings to inform future grants.

- Fund a book on blended learning and work with the author to get the book commercially published and distributed.

Many foundations like to invest in the operation of actual schools. While the price tag on starting a new school from scratch can run into seven figures (see the lists of larger investments below), there are also more economical ways to fund blended learning in classrooms near you:

- Support a pilot program in a few classrooms at a school that's amenable to innovation. Supplement existing technology, and pay for someone to help the teachers select software. This grant might also underwrite the training of teachers, and some uncomplicated data collection on teacher satisfaction, student and parent satisfaction, and student test scores.

- Find a school that already has a plan for transitioning to a blended-learning model, and fund practical requirements like teacher training, beefed-up internet wiring, or other needs.

- Fund the creation of a learning lab on a whole-school level, if a school agrees to try a comprehensive blended model. An investment on the order of $100,000 could pay for supplemental technology to augment what the school already has, plus software, plus tech support or instructional assistants.

- Fund a summer-school blended-learning program for at-risk students who've failed a math class during the year, or a summer enrichment program for students who need stiffer challenges in math. Because blended learning naturally differentiates, this could be the same program.

- Fund a supplemental after-school blended-learning program, and track the results.

- Support the creation of an alternative flex-model program at a high school, in which students mostly take classes online but receive some tutoring from teachers and instructional aides. This program could

Incorporating Blended Learning into Your Broader K–12 Strategy

Whether you pursue a blended-learning strategy explicitly or not, blended learning can inform other giving priorities. Says Luis de la Fuente of Broad Foundation funder Eli Broad, "Every time he talks to anybody about anything, blended learning comes up." And so "we're really weaving it into more and more of everything that we do."

The Broad Foundation runs a superintendents academy, and these education leaders now all do a session on blended learning. Even though the Walton Family Foundation doesn't fund much digital education directly, it has become a part of their strategy for funding lots of charter-school startups. Likewise, as part of its focus on turning around failed schools, the CityBridge Foundation uses blended learning as one important tool.

If you support education research, you can support research into blended learning as part of that. If you support a charter school in your region, you can encourage the school leader to investigate the technology that's out there. In the future, it will be difficult for active school-reform philanthropists to proceed without at least some role in their strategy for computerized instruction.

primarily serve students who want an alternative to traditional school structures because of work or family commitments, disability, disciplinary infractions, or other reasons.

- Pay for a consultant to work with a school or two on exploring blended-learning options. Even if no one's ready to create a pilot right now, this investment in knowledge and familiarity may pay off over time.

- Pay for teachers to take classes (as soon as they exist—see those proposed on pages 111–112) in the best forms of digital-learning instruction.

If you are interested in *policy initiatives* in particular, there are important advances that could be funded for an investment in the $50,000–$100,000 range:

- Undertake a study of your state's laws to see if any are hindering the introduction of blended learning. Share the results with legislators. iNACOL has worked with most of the states to look at their policies, but yours might not be among them.

- Fund the writing of model legislation that would support the shift to mastery-based learning instead of seat-time, and that would be supportive of blended learning more broadly.

- Support a state digital-learning plan. Remind your state's leaders that states have committed to transitioning very soon to online assessments, which will require investments in computers and software—making this an opportune moment to consider blended learning as part of a broader digital-access plan.

If you're open to higher-risk strategies, there are small investments that could potentially create major returns down the road:

- A $25,000 grant might support an educational entrepreneur for six months as he or she produced a business plan for a new school, an operational efficiency in an existing school, or a new ed-tech product. "You have a lot of people who do scaling type of work, but not many who will help entrepreneurs get started," says Luis de la Fuente of the Broad Foundation. Sometimes truly innovative educational ideas "need a little bit more runway than a traditional incubator gives them," says Alan Louie of Imagine K–12. Funding the creative work of an independent visionary at an early stage is not for neophytes, but it can sometimes produce a very big bang for the buck. Consider making several of these investments, knowing that only one or two are likely to pan out.

- A handful of $25,000 grants could produce an educational fellows program that would support multiple entrepreneurs, who could also provide feedback on each other's models and products. There would be lots of ways to structure such a program. You could run it yourself and have candidates apply to you. You could fund positions at an educational think tank. You could give grants to an educational incubator.

> If you're open to higher-risk strategies, some small investments could potentially create major returns down the road.

- Organize a start-up weekend, where school leaders gather to discuss new models and then vote on the best. Award a prize to the winner, and potentially partner with someone else to arrange implementation funds.

- Fund a prize competition for local school districts or for charter-school networks willing to set up blended-learning pilots within their systems.

- If, in the competition above, you get a great plan from an organization willing to translate it into reality, have a second stage of the competition where you partner with the winner to help implement the plan.

- Fund "come-and-see" events for skeptical teachers to observe up close, without pressure, how blended learning works. If teachers are resistant, a school's experiment in blended learning is unlikely to succeed, so dealing with concerns before there are actual proposals on the table can lay essential groundwork.

Giving in the Range Up to $500,000

Investments of this size make more ideas possible. You can multiply any of the previous opportunities—funding multiple pilot programs, for instance—or expand their scope. Some additional possibilities:

- Fund a short course to train teachers and administrators from multiple schools in digital-learning strategies. This course could itself be blended: partially online, with a face-to-face component. The Connelly Foundation funds a Summer Tech Academy for teachers at Philadelphia-area Catholic schools. It started with five figures of annual funding and have now expanded the program to train 180 teachers at a six-figure annual cost.

- Inform teachers. There is relatively little information on what effective technology-enhanced teaching looks like. A funder might pay for the creation of an authoritative handbook or online archive compiling the best techniques and strategies.

- Translate that handbook and archive of effective blended-teaching techniques into a training program for teachers, either live or online.

- Launch a teacher-focused platform to help educators create experiments (or replicate ones others have done) and share the results. This virtual faculty room would provide lesson plans, videos, and other resources.

- Fund blended-learning research and development. Work with blended schools to document which software works best with different students, which class configurations work best, what homework best supports in-class gains, what formats teachers should see data in, what interventions should be pursued first when the data show problems, and so forth. Build support for evidence-based teaching.

- There are currently a handful of good support organizations (like Education Elements and New Classrooms) that are in business to help schools make the jump to blended learning, and help teachers implement new forms of instruction. This field of implementation consultants will need to expand rapidly if hundreds of schools are to transition to blended learning. A funder might help expand these organizations, create new ones, or simply give groups of schools the money to contract with them.

- Fund an organization that can produce objective, detailed reviews of the strengths and weaknesses of software programs and other educational technology offerings. Publish and share these findings with educators who need to make informed decisions when equipping classrooms.

- Work with existing institutions such as the Council of Chief State School Officers or the National Association of School Boards of Education to train their members to understand and work with blended schools.

- Go to one of the various business incubator or seed-funding programs mentioned earlier and help one of their promising young education-technology companies launch themselves as a full-fledged commercial operation. Funding in the range of $250,000 might achieve this.

- Support academics who will do traditional, longer research projects on blended learning (the kind published in peer-reviewed journals).

- Fund the operations of advocacy groups operating on a national level to promote blended learning: iNACOL, Innosight Institute, Alliance for Excellent Education, Foundation for Excellence in Education, Digital Learning Now, or others.

- Support the work of technology incubators that have a track record of spinning out thoughtful ed-tech start-ups.

- Bring together ed-tech entrepreneurs and educators and researchers (particularly those focused on the Common Core or high standards in general) in order to encourage the inclusion of high-quality blended learning in new curricula as they are developed.

- Help your state roll out its plan for computerized annual testing, with an eye toward using this timeline to advance blended learning more broadly.

- Support a series of regional conferences on blended learning aimed at teachers and school leaders. Help educators network and share best practices.

- Fund testing experts with the aim of improving the examinations used to find out how much a student has learned in a course or during a year. Current assessments can sometimes miss the valuable back-filling of knowledge gaps that mastery-based digital instruction is effective at exposing and filling in.

- Fund a statewide conference tied to a grant competition, administered through the state department of education and ideally championed by the governor, to support a blended-learning program and raise awareness.

- Partner with other foundations or public funding sources to start a blended-learning school in your community, or transform an existing school. While $500,000 won't pay for a building, it could pay for the technology, curricula, and the planning and launch of such an institution.

Giving $1 Million or More

- Start a new school. This is generally the price point for full-blown creation of a new institution—or partnering with other groups to create a handful of schools in a portfolio approach. The Rogers Family Foundation has given about this amount to create four pilot programs at schools in Oakland, which the foundation will then study for student results and teacher satisfaction.

• Contribute to an investment pool (like the Silicon Schools Fund, Charter School Growth Fund, or NewSchools Venture Fund) dedicated to the launch of new blended-learning schools, expansion of existing school networks, or support of other educational organizations or companies that undergird blended learning. Since more such funds will eventually be needed, one might also create a new pooled fund.

• Fund runners-up from other grant competitions, so these programs can be launched in the real world. Someone else has already vetted these models, and just because one wasn't the top scorer doesn't mean it isn't good.

• Support 8–10 different states or school districts as they develop blended-learning strategies.

• Make your own direct grant to a successful blended-learning operator to help that organization expand its operation to additional students in new parts of the country. Seven-figure investments in expansion are usually staggered over several years, with built-in growth and performance targets.

One particularly innovative way to use $1 million? Rethink the way schools assess knowledge.

• Tom Vander Ark suggests creating a merit badge system, probably aligned to the Common Core curriculum, that shows proven competence in specific areas. The development of a trusted merit-badge system would give pupils proof of what they could do for potential employers, and move schools toward a system of mastery-based assessment. High school completion could eventually be transformed into the completion of 250 badges, with no immutable time expectation on earning them.

• Collaborate with a school or small school district to implement such a merit-badge system as an alternative graduation path. This would require working with state education officials and local employers and colleges as well. One option would be to build a trial system for use by home schoolers, which could eventually be adopted system wide.

- Support the independent design of a mastery-based curriculum and assessment program, potentially looking to successful existing commercial providers like Kumon and Sylvan Learning for examples and inspiration.

Other eclectic ideas:

- Fund a documentary film supporting blended learning, to raise public awareness and build political pressure. Foundations funded *Waiting for Superman.* "If you want to get to the public, movies are a pretty good way to do it," says de la Fuente.

- Influence television producers, journalists, even companies that sell school supplies to weave blended-learning references into their storytelling and advertising narratives.

- Fund a statewide ballot initiative in support of blended learning and correlated education reform (see the caveats, below, on funding political action).

- Work with an amenable school of education at a major university to create a certificate program in blended learning, or to have blended-learning techniques woven into broader training in pedagogy. "Just because a 23-year-old came into teacher preparation wired doesn't mean they can teach with these tools," says Bob Wise. "For a funder who wants to take it on, it's hard work, but there are some teacher colleges that are willing to try."

- Support a new-format education school, such as the Relay Graduate School of Education, which will train teachers in blended-learning techniques.

- Contribute to a national image-raising campaign that publicizes blended learning through advertising, much as dairy farmers or air traffic controllers have burnished public understanding and appreciation of their industries through public-relations campaigns.

Caveats and Questions

Grantmaking is seldom an exact science, and funders who've supported blended learning in the past mention several lessons they've learned in the process.

Don't force blended learning on anyone. If a school leader is reticent, the experiment has a high chance of failing. Well-designed pilots are at least partially opt-in: the teachers choose to participate, and parents can move children to different classes in the case of objections. Likewise, don't force your choice of software on a school. You can advise, but schools need to own the process.

Don't expect site visits alone to sell blended learning. Site visits raise awareness and answer many questions, but seeing 40 kids in a classroom staring into their MacBooks will not immediately cause an educator to go out and launch a blended-learning school. Site visits are best used as part of a multi-pronged strategy for getting people excited about blended learning.

When in doubt, try a contest. A well-thought-through request for proposals helps you clarify the aims of your giving. A contest creates a whole cohort of organizations going through creative rethinking. They can support and learn from each other and build regional momentum, even outside the institutions that actually win. Plus, the competitive dynamic of a contest is a motivation in its own right. "Race to the Top has been a really brilliant construct," says Deb Quazzo of GSV Advisors. "It's created progressive behaviors in districts because they really want the money." Race to the Top shows that "peer pressure really works and incentives really work."

Don't reinvent the wheel. Before launching a new school, see if an existing model could be adapted with tweaking. While funding a completely new institution can be a worthy endeavor, there's no point creating a new Carpe Diem without benefiting from the lessons Carpe Diem has learned. This is one good reason not to skimp on the planning phase of any project.

Be brave. Many philanthropists say they want to fund "proven strategies" but in a brand new field, there aren't many proven strategies. You could, instead, fund "proven people" who've launched other education programs and have shown how they learn from the experience. "Starting schools is inherently complicated," says Scott Benson of the Bill & Melinda Gates Foundation. "My advice is to be diligent that the person you're backing has the capacity to manage through the complexity that's inherent to this process. Starting a charter that's innovating on an instructional model requires a degree of leadership that extends beyond what it requires to start up a traditional charter school."

Be entrepreneurial. Even donors who were previously intrepid businessmen often turn timid, risk-averse, and bureaucratic in their philanthropy. "I would ask the foundations of this world, the donors, to adopt a 21st-century, entrepreneurial mindset," says donor Dan Peters. Many slow-moving foundations tell potential grantees, "Send us a great big proposal. We meet four times per year. And we need three copies." Instead, funders ought to share "a sense of urgency" with potential problem solvers, and be "flexible in giving." When Peters funded the planning of Carpe Diem's expansion to Indianapolis, "I didn't ask them for an end-of-year report. Their end-of-year report is that they opened Indianapolis. They either did it or they didn't. Eight months later the guy has a fully functioning classroom open in Indiana. If that's not success, I don't know what is."

Focus your support on places where new thinking can be walled off from old thinking. In any bureaucracy, innovators can easily be distracted or obstructed. The authors of *The Innovator's Dilemma* suggest these practical measures to make sure fresh thinking doesn't get suffocated: Keep the innovation teams small and protected from the rest of the organization. Support experimentation. Don't wait for perfect ideas, just find starting points that can be improved rapidly. Make sure you find grantees who understand the importance of trying new things.

Don't accept trivial improvements. At least initially, seek and expect big gains like one and a half years of measured math or literacy growth in a single school year. New-form schools should greatly improve upon low-quality alternatives, or they won't be worth the effort required to push them through.

Think a lot about think about measurement and evaluation. Demonstrated improvements in academic achievement are the goal. But also factor in economics. Scott Benson of the Gates Foundation urges funders to consider "learning growth per dollar invested. And that dollar invested needs to include amortized costs and upfront costs as well as the ongoing expenses of implementation."

Stay informed. Keep in close contact with other funders to avoid duplicating each other's efforts. That said, don't be too worried if there are others operating in the same field. "The more funding opportunities that we have nationally and in individual states and individual districts or communities, the better," says John Fisher, head of the Doris and Donald Fisher Fund, which has invested in the Silicon Schools Fund and also replication vehicles like the Charter School Growth Fund. "Education reform needs a thousand flowers to bloom, not three."

Details matter. Expect your grant recipients to be able to explain and justify nitty-gritty operations, and how they will serve the new model. "Ask any school leaders you're considering funding to explain details of the school day in plain language," urges Brian Greenberg of the Silicon Schools Fund. "It's literally about bell schedules and teacher assignments, it's that level of fine-tuning. And if they can't explain it to you in a way that makes sense, then they don't understand it well enough to be betting on them right now."

Picture your exit strategy. If a blended-learning school or program can't support itself on regular operating funds after five years, it's probably not replicable.

Don't just buy machines. While plenty of schools would love (and perhaps need) better computers or iPads, "so often, you give a bunch of computers to a school and nothing happens," says former Los Angeles Mayor Richard Riordan. "Every school that comes after us for money is doing 'blended learning,' but they're really not. They have no idea what it is." So before making grants, "we actually go in and get a feel, a good intelligent feel, to see if they're actually going to do what they say." Investigate. Just because a school calls its program "blended learning" doesn't mean it will be transformative.

Don't underinvest in IT support. If the software doesn't work on the first day of a blended-learning pilot, there may not be a second day.

Talent matters. The skill level of companies you work with to provide technology-related products or services matters enormously—and differs widely. "We've learned that technical talent is scarce and the difference between top technical talent and mediocre is maybe 20 times," explains Jennifer Carolan of the NewSchools Venture Fund, who was paraphrasing a quote from Steve Jobs. "It can mean all the difference." And quite apart from the technology issues, it's important to work with partners who know what they're doing. Public relations, for instance, can be done poorly or done well, depending on the knowledge and relationships of the firm engaged. Policy wisdom is also important. Make sure your grantees understand the differences between operating in places like California versus Massachusetts—where rules differ widely, and per pupil annual financial allotments can vary by as much as two to one.

Expect a mess. Creating something new is often complicated. It's okay to experience failures if you learn from those experiences. Knowing what not to do—and making sure other people know it—is valuable in its own right. "I don't think we're getting the rapid innovation we could have if there was a little bit more support to try something that might not be perfect the first time. If you are not immediately successful, or don't do something off the charts, it may still have been worth the investment," suggests Christopher Rush of New Classrooms.

Have fun. "Most effective philanthropy starts with philanthropists doing something that they love," says Fisher. If you love technology, funding accelerators and incubators might make you happier than funding schools. On the other hand, if you love visiting with kids and teachers in a cafeteria, a school is the way to go. And be sure to leave room for serendipity. Khan Academy didn't necessarily fit in the planned Gates Foundation education giving strategy, but Bill Gates used it for his own kids. You never know when you'll stumble across something you love and will want to fund it—even if it doesn't strictly stick with the plan.

Bold philanthropy funds "proven people," rather than just funding proven strategies.

On three broader questions that funders must consider—getting involved in politics, paying for content, and funding experiments within traditional school districts—philanthropists have pronounced differences of opinion. We will look at each of these sticky issues in turn.

Should Philanthropists Fund Political Action?

Some donors and educational entrepreneurs argue that foundations should not shy away from funding policy changes—which often means lobbying and working through the political process. "Public education is very political," says John Danner of Rocketship Education. "We can't just build good companies and products and operations and expect the thing to solve itself." Many people at foundations feel that "politics is dirty and messy and they don't want anything to do with it." But if you feel that way, "then you probably shouldn't give too much in public education."

One approach: "When you get these cities or states that are currently forward-leaning, you need to try to keep the forward-leaning people in office. We need to keep in office incumbents who take political risks to accomplish things." Former Washington, D.C., Mayor Adrian Fenty "is the worst example for us," bemoans Danner. "He staked his political career on taking educational risks, and the union put a million dollars against him. Our side put up a couple hundred thousand." Fenty lost his campaign for re-election. "That needs to not happen. Elected officials are pretty rational."

Individual donors interested in education reform could, in theory, work toward getting Republican majorities in state houses, because Republicans have generally been more aligned with the cause of education reform than Democrats. But in terms of passing broad, bipartisan legislation, encouraging Democrats to support, or at least accept, school reform will sometimes be the more consequential achievement. That's what makes organizations like Democrats for Education Reform (DFER) intriguing. Its mission is to champion Democratic legislators who are willing to promote reform despite deep resistance in their party. As executive director Joe Williams puts it, it tries to make education reform a neutral issue for Democrats, rather than one that's "all risk and no reward at this point."

"What we try to do is get it to a draw, so Democrats can decide for themselves if it's a good idea or not, and feel something other than just pain" if they support reform, or at least don't block it. Inertia may be the biggest enemy of all, according to Williams. Opponents of education reform can be "extremely powerful when convincing people not to do anything."

There are of course legal strictures that block nonprofit 501(c)(3) foundations from engaging heavily in direct lobbying. And political advocacy, politi-

> Most effective philanthropy starts with philanthropists doing something that they love.

cal endorsements or opposition, and donating time or money to campaigns are forbidden. If you're willing to think a little differently, though, philanthropists aren't completely blocked from political action.

In addition to donating to groups such as DFER that take on the political blocking and tackling, living donors who are passionate about this topic and recognize the importance of politics can make taxable political donations as individuals. They also can set up parallel 501(c)(4) organizations, which are not tax-deductible, but can engage in unlimited lobbying related to their mission, as well as being free to engage in political activity, endorsements, and campaign donations.

Donors often don't have to give that much. As Danner points out, "the difference between a progressive school district and a recalcitrant one can be a couple of board members." If your foundation is focused locally, and a few school board members are closed-minded about reform, even modest spending can have a big impact on local elections. It's important to do this in smart ways, for instance by rallying parents to the cause of reform as well as making targeted donations. While a local politician might run successfully against a meddling millionaire who's trying to "buy" an election, it's harder to run against hundreds of organized families.

Parents whose children attend Rocketship schools formed a political action committee (PAC) and in 2010 ran four candidates for the local school board. Three of these four candidates won with help from the parents who staffed phone banks and got out and talked to their neighbors. "These elections are won or lost by 1,000 votes," says Danner. "Ten thousand dollars matters. That probably will not always be the case. But right now it's an easy opportunity."

Should Philanthropists Fund Specific Content Like Software Programs?

Another big question is whether foundations should fund the creation of software or educational content. Given how many school leaders complain about the mediocre quality of content that's currently available, and the paucity of useable dashboards that unify results from different programs, this seems like an area where philanthropists could make a difference.

Perhaps it could be—and some foundations are indeed making investments here. The Gates Foundation has given money to Khan Academy, Rocketship, and other schools to build electronic platforms that allow multiple content sources to work together. Some school leaders like Rick Ogston at Carpe Diem have encouraged foundations to think about working directly with software companies to create more interchangeability, so blended-learning schools could plug many varieties of content into their computerized curricula and get useful results in a standard format.

There are reasons to believe that market incentives aren't functioning perfectly in the area of educational software. In theory, the educational market should be swimming with eager entrants, all competing with each other to offer excellent products to schools. After all, it's a huge market: 50 million kids in grades K–12. These consumers are young and impressionable, so garnering their loyalty could have lifelong ramifications.

As GSV Advisors discovered from their market survey, there's no shortage of capital available to fund ed-tech companies. There are, however, other blockages in the system. A major problem is that the purchasing process for educational software is often difficult for both program-writing companies and new schools to navigate. It can take years to conclude a major sale. The buyers aren't the end users. In many school districts, dozens of people are empowered to say "no" to a given deal, but few are empowered to say "yes." These and other obstacles poison entrepreneurial decisiveness. And because school bureaucracies can be so cumbersome to work with, tech companies may not consult with educators in advance as deeply as would be ideal, or beta-test with them as much once a program has been written. That can result in quality problems.

Because of the difficulties of working with school districts, ed-tech companies are increasingly reaching out directly to final consumers. They are selling to students, parents, and teachers, aiming to get them hooked on their productivity-enhancing tools so that there is grassroots-user pressure to bring them in the front door of the school. Engrade, a suite of grading, attendance, calendar, and reporting tools, has been adopted virally by a large percentage of New York City teachers, for instance. It received initial funding through a philanthropic investment by the NewSchools Venture Fund.

The Ed-Tech Market Map, funded by the Laura and John Arnold Foundation and created by Anthony Kim and Michael Horn for the NewSchools Venture Fund, found in 2011 that private capital and companies serve some segments of the educational software market better than others. Plenty of products cover elementary school math. Fewer products are good at training teachers or making them more productive.

A number of ed-tech experts argue that there is a need to expand the whole ecosystem by making it easier for experienced educators to become entrepreneurs. "The real hole is in early-stage stuff," says Heather Gilchrist of Socratic Labs. Since content will generally be better if educators are involved, the work of firms like 4.0 Schools is particularly important, she says. "What they're doing—taking educators who are maybe Teach For America alums, and already kind of entrepreneurial by nature, and helping them now segue from educator to education entrepreneur—that's the really important first step."

Deb Quazzo of GSV Advisors argues that philanthropists might help encourage a handful of the right kind of educational professionals to migrate into commercial product development. More generally, donors might make efforts to increase the flow of ideas, technology, and people across the divides now separating the educational and business worlds. Improved matchmaking and creating forums for sharing technology among the separate worlds of research, business, and classroom practice could strengthen education technology without the dangers of distorting the market that could arise from, for instance, philanthropists bankrolling specific technologies or companies.

> Because of the difficulties of working with school districts, ed-tech companies are increasingly reaching out directly to final consumers.

Another way foundation money could improve content options is to keep content free wherever possible—as happened with Khan Academy products after a few philanthropies stepped in. Because Khan Academy is available today at no cost, schools or teachers can experiment with it while avoiding all the purchasing headaches associated with fee-based products. Sidestepping the need to get official approval is often crucial to working innovations quickly into classrooms, as teachers adopt new products in a viral fashion, much like they integrated Facebook into their personal lives.

On the other hand, a product doesn't have to be supported by philanthropy to be free to the end consumer. There is no reason to be harshly hostile to advertising. Google is in schools and used heavily, and Google relies principally on paid ads. "There are alternative business models where the end user is not necessarily the payer," says Alan Louie.

Philanthropists should also keep in mind that free content can sometimes crowd other things out of the market in ways that are unfortunate. Not everyone will want to use Khan Academy—which doesn't cover all subjects, or at the particular level that teachers might desire, and which requires bandwidth-hogging video streaming. The educational market, like others, is best served by having lots of options and competition. The last thing a donor would want to do is prevent other Sal Khans who have great ideas for helping kids from starting new companies because they have to compete with an entrenched, philanthropy-subsidized entity that is free.

For these sorts of reasons, many observers caution that investing in software is the sort of thing that venture capitalists, or established publishers, may do better than donors. Jim Blew of the Walton Family Foundation says that "philanthropy does not have a great history of choosing technological winners. People who do that—like venture capitalists—do it for a living. They take a lot of risks and suffer the consequences. None of that happens in philanthropy." In fact, misguided philanthropy can keep alive programs that otherwise wouldn't survive, which greatly confuses the market.

In addition, it's usually best not to anoint a single solution, because different content will work for different kids. Teacher Wendy Chaves reports that her Los Angeles students at ATAMS reacted poorly to the Sal Khan videos, for instance, for a variety of cultural reasons.

Philanthropy may also lack the speed and nimbleness to churn out timely products. John Danner, who knows something about making money in software from his Silicon Valley career prior to co-founding Rocketship, notes that "the thing about technology is that once the market incentives start to work," and once investors start seeing people make money, "they'll move a hundred times faster" than anyone in the traditional education world would.

Gisèle Huff of the Jaquelin Hume Foundation agrees that while much current content is sub-par, "the content is going to improve, exponentially, day by day, independently of any donor's money." The market, she says, "will shake this out. There's no way philanthropy can make good bets."

The general consensus is that what philanthropy can most usefully do is build a big market for intelligent products. If there are enough schools demanding good blended-learning programs, entrepreneurs will appear to serve them. Boost demand, the argument goes, and supply will appear.

One can do this by creating new schools and programs, and also by supplementing the technology budgets of schools that already exist (as long as software is purchased as part of a well-thought-through blended-learning strategy). "Education does not work as a normal marketplace," states Jim Blew, because of the government monopoly in most places. The "solution isn't investing in technology," though. "It's investing in making our education system work more like every other aspect of the American economy."

One alternative for donors with an interest in improving the quality of educational software might be fund groups that evaluate and rate software. In New York City, for instance, a group called CFY helps teachers, parents, and students assess and understand different programs. They are partially funded by the Broad Foundation and others. Some groups are working on easily understood ratings systems like the reviews on Amazon. Donors could help encourage this.

Another way for philanthropists to help schools make sense of content options is to support hand-holding groups like Education Elements. These organizations not only advise schools on how to choose great content, but can also provide a single-login structure that allows students and teachers to access all the programs and data through one system, even smoothing certain incompatibilities between content providers. Many donors have chosen to pay Education Elements or some similar consultancy to help schools set up their blended-learning computer systems.

One massive philanthropy-driven project is aimed at establishing a technical base that will ease the transition toward digital learning. An organization called inBloom is now rolling out nationwide the computer infrastructure needed to make data on individual student achievement consistent and comparable across the country, and able to be matched with information on what content and curricula the pupils were using before they got those results. Currently that information exists in wildly different formats and locations that don't integrate with one another. This huge technological undertaking, which should ease many of the operational hitches that now slow the adoption of blended learning, was funded by the Carnegie Corporation and the Gates Foundation.

The inBloom infrastructure will make it possible to read the "story" of how real children progress or languish in digital-learning programs. The technology includes middleware that helps different networks talk to each other, a secure cloud repository where all records can be stored, dashboards that

Observers caution that investing in software is the sort of thing that venture capitalists may do better than donors.

translate student data into manageable and easily understood forms, maps that graphically represent results to help educators see student achievements and needs, and software tools that will enable ed-tech vendors and developers to create programs that can talk with each other. With these tools now being released, it will soon be possible for states, districts, and individual schools to match up inputs and outcomes and be much more systematic about how they pursue blended learning.

Should Foundations Work with Traditional School Districts?

Much of the innovation happening in blended learning is taking place in charter schools—mostly because they're often smaller and more responsive, and more open to doing different things. Scott Benson from the Gates Foundation warns that "change is hard" and "trying to eliminate the notion of courses and grades and traditional class-size ratios" within a school with traditional governance structures is triply hard. "What we're struggling with is that if you want to create a lot of innovative models, the best place to start is where you're not constrained by legacy systems."

That either means working in complete turnaround schools—places that have been shut down and reopened by regulators because they were performing so miserably—or else creating new schools, which in general means a charter school. Yet boutique innovators like "KIPP alone are not going to solve the educational crisis in this country," notes Benson. The biggest reason to consider working with traditional school districts is the simplest one: that's where most of the kids are.

This is precisely why ed-tech companies focus on traditional schools. EdModo, a sort of Facebook for students, serves more than 11 million teachers and students globally, most of whom are not in charter schools. Knewton COO David Liu reports that the major customers for his adaptive-learning software are the McGraw-Hills and Pearsons of the world—content publishers with deep reach into traditional schools. From the commercial ed-tech side, digital learning is not particularly a charter-school phenomenon, and probably never will be.

As a new generation of students and teachers view technology as normal and obvious, technology-enhanced practices are already infiltrating regular classrooms. While working with old-line school boards and district leaders can be frustrating, the way things are now is not necessarily the way things will always be. Philanthropists can nudge districts to try something new.

"A small family foundation—let's say in Tennessee, or Ohio—could fund a one-day summit and give an overview of blended learning, some examples, some best practices, and give out $10,000 to $20,000" in grants, suggests Susan Patrick, the president of iNACOL. "School districts want to do this. They just need a little incentive as political cover. A small grant like that is perfect."

About a third of the recipients of Next Generation Learning Challenges grants (funded by Hewlett, Gates, and other foundations) were district schools. The Silicon Schools Fund grantee criteria leave open the possibility of district schools receiving funds, with John Fisher calling himself cautiously optimistic on that idea. "I think much of it depends on the sort of governance structures that exist and whether Silicon Schools Fund can get comfortable that there's going to be enough independence and autonomy resting with the school leader that he or she will be able to implement the right strategy for the school unencumbered by red tape and bureaucracy," says Fisher.

"I guess my feeling about that," he continues, "is that we have a lot of districts, large and small, in the Bay Area. And I think we have certain mayors and superintendents who would be excited to be a place that was known as a center for the next generation of learning and the next generation of schools." So there is at least some possibility of finding partners within the ranks of traditional school districts. From the Rogers Family Foundation–funded blended-learning pilots in Oakland to Rhode Island's statewide initiatives, there are clearly traditional schools willing to entertain the possibility of innovation. Smart philanthropists will find these willing partners, and find ways to encourage them.

CONCLUSION

Is This Time Really Different?

Education reformers have scars from years of lurching from one trendy idea to the next. Teach For America founder Wendy Kopp writes in her book, *A Chance to Make History*, that there are neither silver-bullet solutions nor "silver scapegoats" in education. As her husband, Richard Barth of KIPP, puts it, "There's a desire for people to think they've found a pixie dust that's going to work for kids." Yet education is too big, messy, and human for magical solutions.

Nothing can solve all of America's educational woes in a single stroke. Simply creating charter schools didn't do it. Recruiting young and energetic teachers alone won't do it. Smaller class sizes disappointed. So did small schools, the Gates Foundation's heavily funded experiment. High-stakes testing hasn't banished failure and mediocrity either.

Donors must likewise recognize that technology in general, and blended learning in particular, won't solve all problems. Instituting an effective blended-learning school requires a strong school leader, so most of the early examples are charter schools where principals have more control over hiring teachers and the construction of a potent school mission than leaders in traditional schools generally do. The district schools that have experimented with blended learning have likewise so far been early adopting types. Would blended learning work well in an environment where a principal is just biding her time, and where teachers are resistant? Likely not. As Ethan Gray of the education-reform network CEE-Trust puts it, "People still matter. I feel like that should be the tagline of blended learning."

But even in mediocre schools, children may be better off if they get a few hours per week in a learning lab. Two hours a day of practice in basic skills—with adaptive software and content presented in an intriguing way—would be better than the warehousing that many children experience in malfunctioning classrooms now. And for children who are more advanced, such technology may offer two hours a day of actual challenge—as opposed to now, when America's underperforming schools, and plenty of middle-of-the-road ones too, seem perfectly willing to let their high-potential brains idle.

In the best-case scenario, digital learning options "provide teachers with the ability to offer a level of individualization never seen before," says Barth. That adds rigor to education's starting point, which is to offer children some confidence that "a believing adult stands behind them—one who has faith in them and their future."

This combination of the advantages of technology and human touch is what has many people excited about blended learning. While it can't solve all problems, says Shantanu Sinha of Khan Academy, "we're seeing glimpses of amazing things. I wouldn't go so far to say this is a panacea that's going to work with every student, but certain students are getting results they never would have imagined before." Even when blended learning isn't implemented perfectly, and isn't all that different from current educational models, a little innovation seems to go a long way.

So that's raising hopes that some deeper innovation can take children even further. It's an exciting time to be investing in education, with many of the nation's biggest foundations coalescing around blended learning as a reform

> Would blended learning work well in an environment where a principal is just biding her time, and where teachers are resistant? Likely not.

that may actually work. "Technology is inexorable," insists blended-learning pioneer Frank Baxter. Thus "technology-enabled education is inevitable," so we'll experience it "this generation rather than the next."

"Within five years it will be really a huge element of all schools—well, not all, but 90 percent of schools," says former L.A. Mayor Richard Riordan. "I predict that with total confidence. Normally, I don't predict things with total confidence."

Certainly technology continues to improve at a pace that boggles the imagination. It's possible that within a few years "we'll just call it learning," says Alex Hernandez of the Charter School Growth Fund, not blended learning. "I'm pretty sure it's going to happen whether people want it to or not."

For the first time in a while, there's a sense within the education-reform movement that we're about to have tools that will enable good teachers to become great. Philanthropy can play a big role in making that happen—in identifying promising ideas, nurturing their growth with smart investments, and spreading them as broadly as possible. If it does, America will come closer than it ever has to a schooling system where all children get the education they deserve.

APPENDIX

Resources Worth Consulting

Books

Some books that give an overview of how technology is changing education:

Disrupting Class (2008). Written by Clayton Christensen and Michael Horn, this seminal book describes the directions and theories behind current education innovation efforts. *Disrupting Class* focuses on transformational uses of technology and applies the theory of disruptive innovation to K–12 education, examining how change is likely to occur even in this innovation-resistant sector.

Education Reform for the Digital Era (2012). Published by the Fordham Institute, this collection of five papers outlines policy issues that reformers must address for digital learning to flourish: the role of the teacher in digital instruction, consistency of quality, the true costs of digital learning, school finance, and governance. The authors conclude that a complete reshaping of the education-reform agenda is needed for digital learning to fulfill its promise. This collection addresses tricky issues including school reimbursement and varied student pace.

Getting Smart: How Digital Learning is Changing the World (2011). Written by Tom Vander Ark, this book traces educational innovation in the United States and abroad. The author details efforts to blend online and onsite learning, highlighting schools and programs that offer personalized digital learning. He identifies four distinctive features:
  • Customized learning: students learn at the right level, pace and mode.
  • Competency-based learning: students progress as they demonstrate mastery.
  • Productive staffing: teachers work together for student success.
  • Expanded opportunity: more access to teachers, content, and courses.

Papers and Reports

The Rise of K–12 Blended Learning (2011). Produced by the Innosight Institute, and a follow-up to *Disrupting Class*, this report begins to delineate various categories of blended learning. It also defines how blended learning is different from full-time online learning, and from schools that merely offer a technology-rich learning environment. This report remains useful for its school profiles, explanations of results and advantages, and discussions of the sector's potential. (http://goo.gl/7vDGJ)

Classifying K–12 Blended Learning (2012). A sequel to "The Rise of K–12 Blended Learning," this report further defines blended learning and clarifies questions from the previous report. The authors move away from the tight parameters that they'd previously used to define blended learning, not wanting to restrict experimentation in the field. (http://goo.gl/2zhnh)

Blended Learning in Practice: Case Studies from Five Leading Schools (2012). The Michael & Susan Dell Foundation commissioned case studies of five different blended-learning schools in order to build a stronger body of research about the practices and results in this field. These look in depth at the operations, instructional model, and finances (down to per-pupil budgets) of several schools profiled here—KIPP Empower Academy in Los Angeles, Summit Public Schools, Alliance College-ready Public Schools, and Rocketship Education—as well as FirstLine Schools in New Orleans, not in this guidebook. (http://goo.gl/yyI9m)

Ten Elements of High-Quality Digital Learning (2010). Led by former Governors Jeb Bush and Bob Wise, Digital Learning Now was one of the first organizations to promote online learning. This paper outlines the elements necessary for sound digital-learning policy. (http://www.digitallearningnow.com/wp-content/uploads/2011/09/Digital-Learning-Now-Report-FINAL1.pdf) DLN promotes legislation that adheres to those principles, and grades states based on how their policies stack up.

"The Online Learning Imperative: A Solution to Three Looming Crises in Education" (2010). This article by former West Virginia Gov. Bob Wise outlines why our education system is in need of big changes. (www.all4ed.org/files/OnlineLearning.pdf) "The current process and infrastructure for educating students in this country cannot sustain itself any longer," notes Wise, who outlines three major reasons why innovative digital learning is needed:
- Demand for high-skill employees is outstripping our current educational system capacity to produce job-ready graduates.
- Local, state, and federal education funding is not keeping up with spending, which requires finding economies in education spending.
- There is a serious shortage of high-quality teachers.

3X for All: Extending the Reach of Education's Best (2009). Written by Public Impact, this report examines how technology can expand the reach of the best teachers. The paper is part of a broader project, called Opportunity Culture, which highlights redesigned teacher roles. (http://www.publicimpact.com/images/stories/3x_for_all-public_impact.pdf)

iNACOL, the International Association of K–12 Online Learning, produces several useful reports annually, like this one: *Fast Facts About Online Learning*, an update on basic facts associated with online learning. (www.inacol.org/press/docs/nacol_fast_facts.pdf)

Keeping Pace With K–12 Online Learning. Published by Evergreen Education Group, this reviews state policies, enrollment data, and trends. (www.kpk12.com)

Profiles in Emerging Models (2011). This paper from the Innosight Institute delineates over 40 schools that are using blended learning in some way, ordering the organizations according to geographic location and method of delivering content. It also surveys technology providers and notes a need for policies that will force vendors to compete based on student performance rather than price. (http://goo.gl/bYx1M)

"Moving from Inputs to Outputs to Outcomes" (2011). This Innosight Institute essay draws attention to the need for policies that center on what students actually achieve. It evaluates whether existing policies are aiding or delaying the development of digital learning. Old criteria like seat-time requirements and teacher certification are criticized as inferior to outcome measures such as content mastery and individual student growth. (http://goo.gl/LCmsS)

"The Fall of the Wall: Capital Flows to Education Innovation" (2012). This 91-page slideshow from GSV Advisors outlines current private investment in education, finding a notable uptick in the past three years, which it credits to improving technology and the ability to reach parents and students directly instead of selling solely through school districts. It argues that there is no lack of capital available for worthy projects, but that unfriendly school-district policies, odd buying cycles, and a disconnection of end-users from purchasing decisions are slowing progress. (http://goo.gl/lvjlj)

"American Revolution 2.0: How Education Innovation is Going to Revitalize America and Transform the U.S. Economy." A broader critique of the problems and opportunities in American public education, with a particular eye to ways that technology can yield opportunities. Also created by GSV Advisors. (http://goo.gl/1ZdOq)

"The Ed-Tech Market Map." Created by Anthony Kim and Michael Horn courtesy of funding from the Laura and John Arnold Foundation, and released at The Philanthropy Roundtable's 2011 meeting in San Francisco, this is a survey of the landscape of technology providers active in creating school curricula. This is a starting point when discussing existing digital educational content, and how donors should work with private firms. The map reveals which subject areas are over-saturated with providers, and identifies areas ripe for private or philanthropic investment. One primary lesson: it is less educational content than teacher development and productivity tools that are in short supply today. (http://www.newschools.org/entrepreneurs/edtechmap)

Email and Blog Resources

BlendedLearningNow.com is an aggregator of the leading blogs, news, research, case studies, and videos. It also provides a useful digital toolkit about starting online learning programs. Geared towards educators, philanthropists, civic leaders, and education reformers.

"Investing in Education Innovation" (2012). Written by Alex Hernandez of the Charter School Growth Fund, this article outlines basic concepts for investing in new methods of schooling. Breaks down investments targeted at seed-incubation, launch, and expansion, and describes which funders are currently active at each level. (http://goo.gl/eChMM)

"Our School System Wants to do Blended Learning. Now What?" (2012). Also written by Alex Hernandez, this article warns how difficult it is for established school districts to innovate, and offers a few suggestions for those willing to try: keep innovation teams small and separate from the rest of the organization, start with a strong though not necessarily perfect idea, and create a short cycle between testing, learning, and repeating. (http://goo.gl/MOhr7)

EdSurge is one of today's best curators of information on education technology. Its weekly email highlights the latest ed-tech tools, practices, events, and trends. They focus more on technology and people than on issues pertaining to reform. (https://www.edsurge.com)

GSV Edu Newsletter is a daily email from GSV Advisors. It lists important news stories on education technology and the education reform movement. Since GSV is a merchant banker for education companies, much of the coverage relates to the growth, financing, and acquisition of education companies. (http://gsvadvisors.com)

Blendmylearning.com is a blog written by classroom teachers, school leaders, and funders to test theories about blended learning and record what works. Contributors include charter schools like Achievement First and E. L. Haynes, as well as funders like the Bill & Melinda Gates Foundation and the Silicon Schools Fund.

Plugged In is a daily digital-learning news digest about what's happening within schools and states, published by iNACOL. Presents headlines and short descriptions of each story from around the country. Compared to the GSV Edu email, this focuses more on policy, thought leadership, on-the-ground school issues, and politics. It also features a "best of the blogs" roundup. (http://www.inacol.org/plugged-in/)

Maximize Potential, a blog kept by Scott Benson of the Gates Foundation provides a useful running list of blended-learning resources—articles, white papers, blogs, books, and school overviews. (http://maximizepotential.org/resources/)

Getting Smart, Tom Vander Ark's blog, offers a list of his 60+ top articles on blended learning. Geared slightly more towards practitioners in the field, Vander Ark's essays focus on new ideas, and this compilation is updated regularly. (http://gettingsmart.com/blog/2012/07/posts-about-blended-learning/)

Videos Depicting Online and Blended Learning

When they first discover blended learning, people inevitably want to see what blended classrooms look like. To address this need, the Jaquelin Hume Foundation and a number of other funders began funding short videos to document these schools and their learning models.

Videos about Blended Learning Generally:

"The Fundamentals of Blended Learning" (6:00). Highlights the basics of blended learning, and explains how blended learning is different from traditional models that are simply technology-rich. Discusses how the common notion of schooling is being redefined to center on personalized instruction for students. Portrays the variety of blended-learning structures, and describes early results and how teachers are adapting. The video is produced by Education Elements, a firm that helps schools design blended-learning classrooms. (http://vimeopro.com/edelements/education-elements)

"The Future of Learning" (7:50). Takes a big-picture look at pathways to learning, and considers weaknesses in traditional learning methods. Produced by 2 Revolutions, a design lab that creates blended-learning pilots. (http://www.youtube.com/watch?v=xoSJ3_dZcm8)

"Fixing Our Schools" (42:00). A news special by journalist Juan Williams, this explores blended-learning schools like Carpe Diem Academy, Florida's virtual-schooling program, and the School of One, which uses a student's funding to pay for an individual technology program. It interviews experts Michael Horn, Joel Klein, and Jeb Bush, and offers a look into the lives of students and teachers involved in digital learning. (http://vimeo.com/47868845)

Videos from Inside Individual Blended-learning Schools:

"Blended Learning for Alliance School Transformation (BLAST)" (5:00). Portrays the Alliance for College-ready Public Schools in Los Angeles, and how its 20 schools are transitioning to blended learning. The video depicts a rotation model, where classes are broken into three segments: direct teacher instruction, small-group project-based collaboration, and online individual learning. (http://vimeo.com/33244413)

"Inside Carpe Diem" Short (1:29) or Long (8:48). These videos showcase one of the nation's first schools to adopt blended learning. Founder Rick Ogston points out that most schools are centered on systems instead of students, and argues that Carpe Diem's method blends the best of technology-based learning with face-to-face instruction. (http://vimeo.com/22935792 or http://vimeo.com/23834061)

"Inside KIPP Empower" (9:12). This video highlights the first KIPP school to adopt blended learning, KIPP Empower Academy, which opened in Los Angeles in 2010. This video directly addresses the criticism that technology in schools will eventually replace teachers. As various instructors explain, technology actually frees up time to focus on the needs of individual students. Outlines the financial benefits of blended learning. Facing an annual state-funding decrease of nearly $200,000, KIPP Empower turned to a blended learning model that allows for 28 students per class. (http://www.kippla.org/empower/Ten-Minute-Video.cfm)

"Phaedrus Blended Learning" (9:47). Phaedrus is a project run by Seton Education Partners that has deployed blended learning at a Catholic school in San Francisco's mission district. Led by Scott Hamilton, a key driver behind KIPP and Teach For America's expansion, Phaedrus aims to use educational technology to substantially reduce operating costs and increase the academic performance of students in Catholic schools. (http://www.youtube.com/watch?v=J7bWeaCz6VY&feature=plcp)

"Rocketeers in Action" (9:45). This video shows how Rocketship Education involves parents in schools and offers students individualized learning via a lab model in which students spend a quarter of their school time at computers honing skills they learned in traditional classes. Describes Rocketship's successful teacher preparation and coaching methods, which rely on instant feedback for instructors from master teachers. (This was made before Rocketship's 2013 announcement that it was moving away from centralized Learning Labs and shifting computers into the classroom.) (http://vimeo.com/30557533)

"Los Altos Unified" (3:01). A look inside fifth- and seventh-grade Khan Academy pilots in California, this video focuses on teachers' experiences using Khan materials in their classrooms. They note that because students are able to progress at their own pace, this tool has been beneficial for both under-performing and high-performing students. (http://www.thegatesnotes.com/Topics/Education/Los-Altos-School-District-Teachers)

INDEX

ABOUT
THE PHILANTHROPY ROUNDTABLE

The Philanthropy Roundtable is America's leading network of charitable donors working to strengthen our free society, uphold donor intent, and protect the freedom to give. Our members include individual philanthropists, families, and private foundations.

Mission

The Philanthropy Roundtable's mission is to foster excellence in philanthropy, to protect philanthropic freedom, to assist donors in achieving their philanthropic intent, and to help donors advance liberty, opportunity, and personal responsibility in America and abroad.

Principles

- Philanthropic freedom is essential to a free society.
- A vibrant private sector generates the wealth that makes philanthropy possible.
- Voluntary private action offers solutions for many of society's most pressing challenges.
- Excellence in philanthropy is measured by results, not by good intentions.
- A respect for donor intent is essential for philanthropic integrity.

Services

World-Class Conferences

The Philanthropy Roundtable connects you with other savvy donors. Held across the nation throughout the year, our meetings assemble grantmakers and experts to develop strategies and solutions for local, state, and national giving. You will hear from innovators in K–12 education, economic opportunity, higher education, national security, and other fields. Our Annual Meeting is the Roundtable's flagship event, gathering the nation's most public-spirited and influential philanthropists for debates, how-to sessions, and discussions on the best ways for private individuals to achieve powerful results through their giving. The Annual Meeting is a stimulating and enjoyable way to meet principled donors seeking the breakthroughs that can solve our nation's greatest challenges.

Breakthrough Groups

Our Breakthrough Groups—focused program areas—build a critical mass of donors around a topic where dramatic results are within reach. Breakthrough Groups become a springboard to help donors achieve lasting results with their philanthropy. Our specialized staff assist grantmakers committed to making careful investments. The Roundtable's K–12 education program is our largest and longest-running Breakthrough Group. This network helps donors zero in on the most promising school reforms. We are the industry-leading convener for philanthropists seeking systemic improvements through competition and parental choice, administrative freedom and accountability, student-centered technology, enhanced teaching and school leadership, and high standards and expectations for students of all backgrounds. We foster productive collaboration among donors of varied ideological perspectives who are united by a devotion to educational excellence.

A Powerful Voice

The Roundtable's public policy project, the Alliance for Charitable Reform (ACR), works to advance the principles and preserve the rights of private giving. ACR educates legislators and policymakers about the central role of charitable giving in American life and the crucial importance of protecting philanthropic freedom—the ability of individuals and private organizations to determine how and where to direct their charitable assets. Active in Washington, D.C., and in the states, ACR protects charitable giving, defends the diversity of charitable causes, and battles intrusive government regulation. We believe that our nation's capacity for private initiative to address problems must not be burdened with costly or crippling constraints.

Protection of Donor Interests

The Philanthropy Roundtable is the leading force in American philanthropy to protect donor intent. Generous givers want assurance that their money will be used for the specific charitable aims and purposes they believe in, not redirected to some other agenda. Unfortunately, donor intent is usually violated in increments, as foundation staff and trustees neglect or misconstrue the founder's values and drift into other purposes. Through education, practical guidance, legislative action, and individual consultation, The Philanthropy Roundtable is active in guarding donor intent. We are happy to advise you on steps you can take to ensure that your mission and goals are protected.

Must-Read Publications

Philanthropy, the Roundtable's quarterly magazine, is packed with beautifully written real-life stories. It offers practical examples, inspiration, detailed information, history, and clear guidance on the differences between giving that is great and giving that disappoints. We also publish a series of guidebooks which provide detailed information on the very best ways to be effective in particular aspects of philanthropy. These guidebooks are compact, brisk, and readable. Most focus on one particular area of giving—for instance, Catholic schools, support for veterans, anti-poverty programs, environmental projects, and technology in education. Real-life examples, hard numbers, management experiences of other donors, recent history, and policy guidance are presented to inform and inspire savvy donors.

Join the Roundtable Today

When working with The Philanthropy Roundtable, members are better equipped to achieve long-lasting success with their charitable giving. Your membership with the Roundtable will make you part of a potent network that understands philanthropy and strengthens our free society. Philanthropy Roundtable members range from *Forbes* 400 individuals and the largest American foundations to small family foundations and donors just beginning their charitable careers. Our members include:

- Individuals and families
- Private foundations
- Community foundations
- Eligible donor advisors
- Corporate giving programs
- Charities which devote more than half of their budget to external grants

Philanthropists who contribute at least $50,000 annually to charitable causes are eligible to become members and register for most Roundtable programs. Roundtable events provide you with a solicitation-free environment.

For more information on The Philanthropy Roundtable or to learn about our individual program areas, please call (202) 822-8333 or email main@ PhilanthropyRoundtable.org.

ABOUT THE AUTHOR

Laura Vanderkam's writing on economics, education, careers, and technology has appeared in the *Wall Street Journal, Reader's Digest, Scientific American, City Journal,* and other publications. She is the author of *168 Hours: You Have More Time Than You Think* and the *What the Most Successful People Do* series of e-books, whose first installment, *What the Most Successful People Do Before Breakfast,* was a number-one audiobook bestseller on iTunes. She is a member of *USAToday*'s board of contributors, and writes the "168 Hours" blog for CBS MoneyWatch. She lives outside Philadelphia with her husband and three children and blogs at LauraVanderkam.com.